Cambridge
of Proficiency ... h
1

WITH ANSWERS

*Examination papers from the
University of Cambridge
Local Examinations Syndicate*

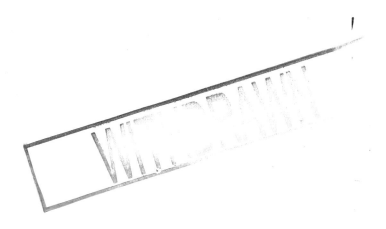

CAMBRIDGE
UNIVERSITY PRESS

PUBLISHED BY THE PRESS SYNDICATE OF THE UNIVERSITY OF CAMBRIDGE
The Pitt Building, Trumpington Street, Cambridge, United Kingdom

CAMBRIDGE UNIVERSITY PRESS
The Edinburgh Building, Cambridge CB2 2RU, UK
40 West 20th Street, New York NY 10011–4211, USA
477 Williamstown Road, Port Melbourne, VIC 3207, Australia
Ruiz de Alarcón, 28014 Madrid, Spain
Dock House, The Waterfront, Cape Town 8001, South Africa

http://www.cambridge.org

First published 2001
Reprinted 2003

Printed in the United Kingdom at the University Press, Cambridge

ISBN 0 521 79993 7 Student's Book
ISBN 0 521 79994 5 Student's Book with answers
ISBN 0 521 00992 8 Self-study Pack
ISBN 0 521 79995 3 Teacher's Book
ISBN 0 521 79996 1 Set of 2 Cassettes
ISBN 0 521 00991 X Set of 2 Audio CDs

Contents

Thanks and acknowledgements

The publishers are grateful to the following for permission to reproduce copyright material. It has not always been possible to identify the sources of all the material used and in such cases the publishers would welcome information from the copyright owners.

Courtesy of Tourism Vancouver for p. 4: an extract from *The Vancouver Book – A Visitor's Guide to Greater Vancouver*; The Random House Group for p. 38: *The Razor's Edge* by Somerset Maugham, published by William Heinneman Ltd. Also for pp. 48–49: extract from *Human Jungle* by Stanton Newman, published by Newbury. Also for p. 61: from *Waterlog* by Roger Deakin, published by Chatto and Windus. Also for p. 96: from *The Human Zoo* by Desmond Morris, published by The Human Zoo. All texts used by permission of The Random House Group. Oldie Publications for p. 5: 'Supermarket Opening' by Alice Pitman; *The Guardian* for p. 6: 'Screen Learning' by Maggie Brown and for p. 75: 'Oops' by Merope Mills and for p. 76: 'Humour in the Workplace' by Anita Chaudri; *The Economist* for p. 7: 'Hollywood', pp. 62–63: 'Online Reviews' and pp. 89–90: 'Garbage in, Garbage Out'; Thames and Hudson Ltd for p. 8: *The Picture History of Photography* by Peter Pollack; Walker Books Ltd for p. 9: *The Telling Line* by Douglas Martin; Piatkus Books for p. 83: *Clear Your Clutter With Feng Shui* by Kate Kingston; *New Scientist* for p. 16: 'Listening to Alex' by Irene Pepperberg; *The Geographical Magazine* for p. 17: 'A Question of Taste' by Chris Hellier; Phaidon Press Ltd for p. 22: reproduced from 'The Story of Art' ©1995 Phaidon Press Limited, text ©1995 E. H. Gombrich; *Contemporary Visual Arts* for p. 23: 'The New, No Longer New Zeitgeist' by Klaus Hobnef, copyright ownership by OPA N.V. Permission granted by Taylor & Francis Ltd; Penguin Books for p. 30: *The Language Instinct* by Steven Pinker; *The Spectator* for p. 31: 'An Art and a Science'; A. P. Watts Ltd on behalf of Graham Swift for p. 33: *The Spirit of the Fens* by Edward Storey; Alexander Hayward for p. 34: 'What is a Museum?'; Little, Brown and Company for pp. 36–37: *Sour Sweet* by Timothy Mo; Michael Chinery for p. 42: *The Natural History of the Garden*; Cambridge University Press for p. 43: *Cambridge Encyclopaedia of Language* by David Crystal, 1987; *Independent* for p. 56: ' Murder Most Moorish' by Paul Taylor; *New Scientist* for p. 56: 'Lake Vostok'; courtesy of *Focus* magazine ©National Magazine Company for p. 57: 'Scientists'; Dominic Lutyen for p. 59: 'Bachelor Fads'; *Gay Times*/James Carey Parkes 2000 for p. 60: 'Bruce Chatwin'; Taylor and Francis Books Ltd for pp. 64–65: *The Photography Handbook* by Terence Wright; Macmillan for pp. 83–84: *Caves* by Tony Waltham; Kingfisher Books for p. 85: 'Looking at Art' by Norbert Lynton; *The Times* for p. 86: 'Picture This' by Waldemar Januszczak; Faber and Faber for p. 88: *Justine* by Lawrence Durrell; pp. 91–92: 'Music and the Ear' by Genista McIntosh (this first appeared in *BBC Music Magazine*, February 2000); *Business Traveller Magazine* for p. 97: 'Every Time We Say Goodbye' by Raj Persaud.

Text permissions by Fiona Donnelly

Colour section photographs: Superstock for p. C2 (1A); Stone for pp. C2 (1B), C3 (1C) and C7 (3E); Science Photolibrary for p. C4 (2A); Telegraph Colour Library/Bavaria-Bildagentur for p. C4 (2B); Stone/Tony Azzura for p. C4 (2C); NPHA for p. C5 (2D); Science Photolibrary/Peter Menzel for p. C5 (2F); Stone/Steve Lewis for p. C5 (2E); Sandra Kennedy for pp. C6 (3A, 3B and 3C) and C7 (3D and 3F); Science Photolibrary/Roger Harris for pp. C8 and C9 (4A).

Picture research by Diane Jones

Cover design by Dunne & Scully

The cassettes which accompany this book were recorded at Studio AVP, London.

To *the* student

This book is for candidates preparing for the University of Cambridge Local Examinations Syndicate (UCLES) Certificate of Proficiency in English (CPE) examination. It contains four complete tests which reflect the most recent CPE specifications (introduced in December 2002).

The CPE is part of a group of examinations developed by UCLES called the Cambridge Main Suite. The Main Suite consists of five examinations which have similar characteristics but which are designed for different levels of English ability. Within the five levels, CPE is at Cambridge Level 5.

Cambridge Level 5 Certificate of Proficiency in English (CPE)
Cambridge Level 4 Certificate in Advanced English (CAE)
Cambridge Level 3 First Certificate in English (FCE)
Cambridge Level 2 Preliminary English Test (PET)
Cambridge Level 1 Key English Test (KET)

The CPE examination consists of five papers:

Paper 1	Reading	1 hour 30 minutes
Paper 2	Writing	2 hours
Paper 3	Use of English	1 hour 30 minutes
Paper 4	Listening	40 minutes (approximately)
Paper 5	Speaking	19 minutes

Paper 1 Reading
This paper consists of four parts with 40 questions, which take the form of three multiple-choice tasks and a gapped text task. Part 1 contains three short texts, Part 2 contains four short texts and Parts 3 and 4 each contain one longer text. The texts are taken from fiction, non-fiction, journals, magazines, newspapers, and promotional and informational materials. This paper is designed to test candidates' ability to understand the meaning of written English at word, phrase, sentence, paragraph and whole text level.

Paper 2   Writing
This paper consists of two writing tasks in a range of formats (e.g. letter, report, review, article, essay, proposal). Candidates are asked to complete two tasks, writing between 300 and 350 words for each. Part 1 (Question 1) consists of one compulsory task based on instructions and a short text. Part 2 (Questions 2–5) consists of one task which candidates select from a choice of four. Question 5 has a task on one of each of three set texts. Assessment is based on achievement of task, range and accuracy of vocabulary and grammatical structures, organisation, content and appropriacy of register and format.

Paper 3   Use of English
This paper consists of five parts with 44 questions. These take the form of an open cloze, a word formation task, gapped sentences, key word transformations and two texts with comprehension questions and a summary writing task. The paper is designed to assess candidates' ability to demonstrate knowledge and control of the language system by completing these tasks which are at text and sentence level.

Paper 4   Listening
This paper consists of four parts with 28 questions, which take the form of two multiple-choice tasks, a sentence-completion task and a three-way matching task. Part 1 contains four short extracts and Parts 2 to 4 each contain one longer text. The texts are audio-recordings based on a variety of sources including interviews, discussions, lectures, conversations and documentary features. The paper is designed to assess candidates' ability to understand the meaning of spoken English, to extract information from a spoken text and to understand speakers' attitudes and opinions.

Paper 5   Speaking
The Speaking Test consists of three parts, which take the form of an interview section, a collaborative task and individual long turns with follow-up discussion. The test is designed to elicit a wide range of language from both candidates. Candidates are examined in pairs by two examiners, an Interlocutor and an Assessor. The Assessor awards a mark based on the following criteria: Grammatical Resource, Lexical Resource, Discourse Management, Pronunciation and Interactive Communication. The Interlocutor provides a global mark for the whole test.

Marks and results

The five CPE papers total 200 marks, after weighting. Each paper is weighted to 40 marks.

A candidate's overall CPE grade is based on the total score gained in all five papers. It is not necessary to achieve a satisfactory level in all five papers in order to pass the examination. Pass grades are A, B or C, with A being the highest. D and E are failing grades. The minimum successful performance in order to achieve Grade C corresponds to about 60% of the total marks. Every candidate is provided with a Statement of Results which includes a graphical display of their performance in each paper. These are shown against the scale Exceptional – Good – Borderline – Weak and indicate the candidate's relative performance in each paper.

The CPE examination is recognised by the majority of British universities for English language entrance requirements.

Further information

For more information about CPE or any other UCLES examination write to:

EFL Information
University of Cambridge Local Examinations Syndicate
1 Hills Road
Cambridge
CB1 2EU
United Kingdom

Tel: +44 1223 553355
Fax: +44 1223 460278
e-mail: efl@ucles.org.uk
http://www.cambridge-efl.org.uk

In some areas, this information can also be obtained from the British Council.

Test 1

PAPER 1   READING (1 hour 30 minutes)

Part 1

For questions **1–18**, read the three texts below and decide which answer (**A, B, C** or **D**) best fits each gap.

Mark your answers **on the separate answer sheet**.

Vancouver

In the last ten years or so, hundreds of thousands of people from all over the world have **(1)** .... up residence in Vancouver, in western Canada. To relax in the evening, residents **(2)** .... down the city streets and, if you join them, you are likely to overhear a different language at almost every other step. People come to Vancouver for its mild climate, its wonderful setting between the ocean and the mountains, its clean and safe environment and its educational and job opportunities. And **(3)** .... some may grumble about the speed at which new buildings have **(4)** ...., there's no doubt that the new arrivals and **(5)** .... tourism industry have helped fuel an urban renaissance. Locals once referred to Vancouver as 'Terminal City' because of the city's role as a terminus or gateway to all other places. Though the name has fallen slightly out of **(6)** ...., Vancouver is more a gateway than ever.

1	**A** taken	**B** put	**C** made	**D** built
2	**A** prowl	**B** stumble	**C** trudge	**D** stroll
3	**A** conversely	**B** nevertheless	**C** much as	**D** even so
4	**A** sprung up	**B** gathered up	**C** piled up	**D** moved up
5	**A** progressing	**B** blooming	**C** flourishing	**D** swelling
6	**A** approval	**B** favour	**C** opinion	**D** support

Putting Pen to Paper

Journalists like myself are usually poor letter-writers. I have heard it **(7)** .... that this is because of the instinctive distaste we feel at writing something we are not going to be paid for, but I cannot believe we have quite such mercenary characters. It is more probably that **(8)** .... in our work, we are always **(9)** .... to get the greatest possible effect, the essential spontaneity of a letter **(10)** .... us. The real creative artist, who does not consciously work on the effect at all (though he may re-write a passage dozens of times), does not have this problem. I believe that it is in this inherent grasp of the effect of his words that there **(11)** .... the only sure test of the real artist. When Shakespeare wrote some of his famous lines he **(12)** .... never thought consciously that it was the contrast between polysyllables that made them so effective, as well as showing him to be a great writer.

7 A	said	**B**	told	**C**	remarked	**D**	presumed
8 A	since	**B**	for	**C**	like	**D**	once
9 A	striving	**B**	exerting	**C**	contending	**D**	tackling
10 A	misses	**B**	escapes	**C**	avoids	**D**	passes
11 A	goes	**B**	remains	**C**	lies	**D**	exists
12 A	inevitably	**B**	confidently	**C**	particularly	**D**	surely

Supermarket Opening

The opening of a new supermarket used to be a bit of an event in Britain. You could always rely on a soap star, a disc jockey or a minor member of the royal family to come down and cut the ribbon. Now it seems that new branches are **(13)** .... up every day in many areas and so the poor old celebrity has become **(14)** .... . Why pay a famous person when any Tom, Dick or Harry will open it for nothing? Last week, waiting pensioners didn't care who opened the new branch of *Superbuy*, **(15)** .... they were at the front. According to one prospective customer who knew someone who worked there, the first five men over the **(16)** .... would be getting a bottle of aftershave, and the first five women, a bunch of flowers. This **(17)** .... of information quickly swept **(18)** .... the crowd, instilling feelings of smug superiority among those at the front, and envy from the latecomers.

13 A	popping	**B**	leaping	**C**	jumping	**D**	nipping
14 A	superfluous	**B**	excessive	**C**	surplus	**D**	residual
15 A	despite	**B**	so long as	**C**	in case	**D**	regardless
16 A	entrance	**B**	doorway	**C**	threshold	**D**	barrier
17 A	clipping	**B**	strand	**C**	string	**D**	snippet
18 A	among	**B**	through	**C**	across	**D**	around

Part 2

You are going to read four extracts which are all concerned in some way with the power of visual images. For questions **19–26**, choose the answer (**A**, **B**, **C** or **D**) which you think fits best according to the text.

Mark your answers **on the separate answer sheet**.

Screen Learning

A few days ago I noticed my six-year-old eating noodles in a funny way. He was pulling them up with his teeth while trying to look fierce. 'I'm a little dinosaur,' he said. He was play-acting a scene from a recent TV programme, so I quizzed him about what he remembered about dinosaurs. The answer was, not a lot.

There is a modish rush to embrace internet and computer learning, but is learning via a screen a good method? One writer tells how he tried out an interactive programme with his son. The father diligently read the words while the son fiddled with the pictures. 'Had he spent ten minutes in front of a book, he might possibly have learned something,' said his father.

Television, as my son and his noodles demonstrate, is an impressionistic, suggestive medium. Research about television and learning shows that learning goes on in a learning environment where dialogue is taking place with teachers or parents. It needs to be mediated. There is nothing wrong with harnessing new technology to teach our children, but there is still a big role for formal education.

19 In order to be used successfully in teaching, TV programmes must

    A   be shown in a conventional classroom.
    B   focus on dialogue.
    C   be accompanied by discussion with adults.
    D   appeal to adults and children.

20 The writer believes that 'screen learning' should be used

    A   with enthusiasm.
    B   in moderation.
    C   without preconceptions.
    D   in isolation.

Hollywood

By 1918, four-fifths of the film-making capacity of the world had relocated to Hollywood. Locals disapproved, seeing their suburb of Los Angeles infected by these new vulgarians. But in the end snobbery yielded to the true American value, success. And success is the box-office gross. Hollywood knows a good film when it sees one: one that may make a star, but must make somebody's fortune.

In less than a century, Hollywood has grown from a toffee-nosed village to a town as famous as New York, Rome or Paris. And physically, of course, it has changed beyond recognition: a century ago, you would walk through orange groves to the village store. Yet in a way, it is still a village – parochial, with limited horizons – just a little bit of Los Angeles. For all who live and work in it, there is one topic of conversation – films: how much they have made, who is dating whom, who's been stabbed in the back, who is 'attached' to which project. Those who have been successful often try to get away: to work there, but live somewhere else. Yet it is still the one place in the world to which almost everyone who is anyone in show-business (and plenty who aren't) eventually   **line 16** gravitates.

21 What does the writer say about present-day Hollywood?

    A The local people still look down on the film industry.
    B It retains some characteristics of a small community.
    C It has been adversely affected by its reputation.
    D People who live there are worried by the violence.

22 Who does 'and plenty who aren't' refer to in line 16?

    A people less well-known in the world of entertainment
    B people not resident in Hollywood
    C people unlikely to achieve celebrity status
    D people not welcome in Hollywood

Photography

Photography was invented by nineteenth century artists as an art form for their own purposes. These men were seeking a lasting, literal record of their visual surroundings and they found it. The new combination of illumination, lens, shutter, and flat surface coated with chemicals sensitive to light produced images more lasting, more convincing in their reality, and more richly detailed than painters could produce manually in weeks and months of effort. This alone was enough to throw consternation into the ranks of fellow artists; and, after their first reaction of pleasure in a new kind of image, art critics rallied with the haughty charge that photography was not, and could not be, an art. The actual world in which we live had too strong a grip on photography, they said, and pictures so dependent upon mechanical means could not be called acts of man's creative imagination.

Despite the critics, photographers knew that they had found a new art form, a new mode of expression. They used the new tools as other artists before and after them have used brush and pencil – to interpret the world, to present a vision of nature and its structure as well as the things and the people in it.

23 What are we told about the artists who first used photography?

    A   They appreciated what photography could offer.
    B   They preferred taking photographs to painting pictures.
    C   They did not want anyone else to benefit from photography.
    D   They thought painting pictures was too arduous.

24 Art critics disapproved of photography because they thought

    A   it needed too little effort to interpret it.
    B   the images were visually displeasing.
    C   it used overly complicated equipment.
    D   it did not go beyond the literal.

Book Illustration

During the black-and-white era of book illustration it was axiomatic that each and every children's book called for some form of illustration. This extended to the large category of novels for the upper reading ages, which was to suffer progressive attrition as print runs shortened. The level of activity in all areas of children's publishing remained considerable, but it was run predominantly as a low-budget operation for most of the period and as such encouraged a fair amount of routine and mediocre work, although the finest artists seldom submitted less than their professional best. Therefore, the black-and-white archive is part junk shop, part treasure house; a wonderful place for research or for browsing, and one in which to make immediate finds or to begin to re-evaluate a fertile artistic period. The real treasures are bound to return to public display, whether enduringly – through re-issues of individual titles and new publications about the artists who illustrated them – or from time to time in the form of exhibitions of original books and drawings. There are signs that, after a period of neglect, this is starting to happen and the familiar processes of stylistic rehabilitation can be seen to be at work. In due course, an enterprising publisher will doubtlessly see the potential for a series of classic children's book illustrations from this period either in facsimile reprint, or in freshly-designed editions using the original artwork where it survives.

25   According to the writer, the constraints of the black-and-white era

   A   produced varying levels of artistic accomplishment.
   B   restricted the categories of books that were illustrated.
   C   meant that artists had to be chosen from a certain calibre.
   D   did not affect the quality of literature produced at that time.

26   Which of the following does the writer predict with confidence?

   A   the production of new black-and-white illustrations
   B   the public's exposure to artwork from the black-and-white era
   C   the resurgence of general interest in black-and-white books
   D   the availability of a wealth of black-and-white original works

Part 3

You are going to read an extract from a novel. Seven paragraphs have been removed from the extract. Choose from the paragraphs **A–H** the one which fits each gap (**27–33**). There is one extra paragraph which you do not need to use.

Mark your answers **on the separate answer sheet**.

In those days the council houses stretched all over the western side of the city: row after row of huddled, dingy dwellings in orange half-brick or pale white stucco. In summer the chemicals from the May and Baker factory two miles away came and hung round the doors and gardens with an indescribable smell of sulphur, and the most common sight in that part of Norwich early in the morning was a paperboy wrinkling his nose in disgust as he negotiated somebody's front path.

27	

That my mother should intrude into these early memories is no surprise. I remember her as a small, precise and nearly always angry woman, the source of whose anger I never quite understood, and consequently couldn't do anything to appease. Even as a child, though, accompanying her to the small shops in Bunnett Square or on longer excursions into the city, I'm sure that I had some notion of the oddity of her personality.

28	

As a moral code this was completely beyond my comprehension: even now I'm not sure that I understand it. To particularise, it meant not straying into neighbours' gardens or jeopardising their rose bushes as you walked down the street; it meant sitting for long half-hours in a silent dining room, with your hands folded across your chest, listening to radio programmes that my mother liked; it meant – oh, a hundred proscriptions and prohibitions.

29	

It was only later that I comprehended what poor company this trio was; they formed a depressed and depressing sisterhood, a little dribble of inconsequent

talk about bad legs, the cold weather and the perils of ingrate children, a category in which I nearly always felt myself included.

30	

This was easier said than done. Growing up in West Earlham at this time followed a well-regulated pattern. Until you were five you simply sat at home and got under your parents' feet (I can remember awful aimless days, when I must have been about four, playing on a rug in the front room while my mother sat frostily in an armchair). Then, the September after your fifth birthday, you were packed off to Avenue Road infants' school half a mile away in the direction of the city.

31	

If I remember anything about these early years it's the summer holidays; those days when you caught occasional glimpses of the world that existed outside West Earlham: a vague old man who lived next door to Mrs Buddery and told stories about his time in the Merchant Navy; a charity fete, once, held at a house far away in Christchurch Road, where a motherly woman doled out lemonade and tried to get me interested in something called the League of Pity – a kind of junior charity, I think – only for my mother, to whom subsequent application was made, to dismiss the scheme on the grounds that its organisers were 'only after your money'.

32	

No doubt I exaggerate. No doubt I ignore her virtues and magnify her frailties. But there was precious little milk of human kindness in my mother; it had all been sucked out of her, sucked out and thrown away.

33	

My mother wasn't, it must be known, altogether averse to this recreation, and eventually almost got to have opinions on the various subjects presented for her edification. I can remember her stopping once in front of a fine study of a Roman soldier in full battle gear to remark, 'Well, I wouldn't like to meet *him* on a dark night!' I recall this as a solitary instance of my mother attempting to make a joke.

A   To do my mother justice she wasn't unconscious of her role as the guardian of my education. On Sundays occasionally, she would take me – in my 'good clothes' – on the 85 bus to the Norwich Castle Museum. Here, hand-in-hand, suspicious, but mindful of the free admission, we would parade through roomfuls of paintings by the Norwich School of Artists.

B   The lucky few had a mother with a rickety bike and a child seat – these were extraordinary contraptions in cast-iron with improvised safety-straps. As far as I recall, my mother consigned me to the care of other children in the street for this journey.

C   Of explanation – who we were, where we came from, what we were supposed to be doing – there was none. And yet it seemed to me that my early life, lived out in the confines of the West Earlham estate, in a dark little house in a fatally misnamed terrace called Bright Road, was crammed with mysteries that demanded explanation. There was, to take the most obvious, the question of my father.

D   She was, for instance, quite the most solitary person I have ever known, as alone in a room full of people as on a moor. To this solitariness was added a fanatic adhesion to a kind of propriety uncommon on the West Earlham estate, which occasionally broke out in furious spring-cleanings or handwashings and instructions to 'behave proper'.

E   Mercenary motives were a familiar theme of my mother's conversation, and politicians my mother held in the deepest contempt of all. If she thought of the House of Commons – and I am not sure if her mind was capable of such an unprecedented leap of the imagination – it was as a kind of opulent post office where plutocrats ripped open letters stuffed with five pound notes sent in by a credulous public.

F   Most of this early life I've forgotten. But there is a memory of sitting, or perhaps balancing, at any rate precariously, on some vantage point near an upstairs window, and looking at the houses as they faded away into the distance. Later on there are other phantoms – faces that I can't put names to, my mother, ironing towels in the back room of a house that I don't think was ours, snow falling over the turrets of the great mansion at Earlham.

G   In time other figures emerged onto these stern early scenes. For all her solitariness, my mother wasn't without her cronies. There was Mrs Buddery, who was fixated on the Royal Family; Mrs Winall, who said exactly nothing, except for grunts supporting the main speaker; and Mrs Laband – livelier than the others, and of whom they vaguely disapproved.

H   Looking back, it was as if a giant paperweight, composed of the West Earlham houses, my mother and her cronies, the obligation to 'behave proper', lay across my shoulders, and that it was my duty immediately to grow up and start the work of prising it free.

Part 4

You are going to read an essay about poetry. For questions **34–40**, choose the answer (**A, B, C** or **D**) which you think fits best according to the text.

Mark your answers **on the separate answer sheet**.

POETRY RECITALS

At any given time in history the literary scene will seem confused to those who are living through it, and it is the selectivity of posterity that makes the pattern and orders of eminence appear clearly defined to the retrospective view. It is fairly safe to say that, at the present time, there is an especially bewildering complexity of poetic tendencies, of kinds of poetry being written, of warring factions, of ways of presenting, criticising and teaching poetry, and of conflicting beliefs about the role of the poet in society.

Very broadly speaking, the present debate in contemporary poetry concerns the reciprocal mistrust and disapproval shown by the seriously committed 'literary' writers, whose poems are intended to be printed and read on the page, and the 'popular', performing poets who, while they will probably publish their verses in magazines and collections, are happier declaiming them to an audience. Of course, this division is far from absolute.

The practice of promoting public poetry readings has been steadily increasing over the past twenty years or so, in many different forms. Small literary societies in provincial towns conduct them in village halls or the sitting rooms of their members; schools and colleges invite poets to read and talk to audiences of students; arts festivals often advertise poetry readings by well-known authors on their programmes. The consequences of all these events, and of poets being more or less obliged to become public performers, are manifold and of uncertain benefit to them as artists.

For the 'pop' poets, whose work has been composed expressly for the purpose of recital to live audiences, the issue is plain. They can only profit from public performance. Their verses are often very simple in both form and content, and can be assimilated at a single hearing; it is on the printed page that the deficences of thought, technique and imagination become clear. Poets who are dedicated to their craft, and are doing their best to continue and develop what is finest in the traditions of poetry – which involves compressing the maximum amount of passion, thought, wit and vision into the smallest possible space and achieving rhythmic effects of great variety and subtlety – are unlikely to be appreciated by an audience which is probably encountering their work for the first time. The danger here is, not that they will be tempted to **line 52** emulate the content and style of the entertainers, **line 53** but that they might, in the effort to achieve instant communication, read only their most readily **line 55** accessible work which is quite likely to be their slightest and least characteristic. **line 57**

Attendance at poetry reading cannot be a substitute for reading poetry on the page, though it can be an enjoyable and instructive adjunct. To hear good poets read their work aloud, even if they are not accomplished public speakers, is a valuable guide as to where the precise emphases are to be placed, but it is desirable that the audience should either follow the reading with the text before them or have a prior knowledge of the poems being spoken. The principal justification for popular recitals of poetry, where the readings are sometimes interspersed with musical items (jazz and poetry used to be a very popular mixture), is that audiences will come to associate poetry with pleasure and not feel that it is an art available only to an initiated minority.

34 What general observation about poetry does the writer make in the opening paragraph?

    A The present literary climate is not conducive to good poetry.
    B Modern poems appear unplanned and chaotic to him.
    C The greatness of poets only emerges in retrospect.
    D Today's poetry compares unfavourably with that of previous generations.

35 What does the writer think about the present conflict in poetry?

    A He blames it on the serious poets.
    B The distinction between 'serious' and 'popular' is seldom clear cut.
    C It stems from the attitude of the audience.
    D The popular poets take pleasure in criticising the serious poets.

36 According to the writer, how might a serious poet feel about a public recital?

    A uneasy about the practical arrangements
    B bound to accept for financial reasons
    C pleased to reach a wider audience
    D under pressure to take part

37 The writer feels that the work of some popular poets

    A does not stand up to close analysis.
    B is part of a long poetic tradition.
    C is undervalued by experienced audiences.
    D benefits from being written down.

38 Which word is used to refer disparagingly to the popular poets?

    A tempted   (line 52)
    B entertainers   (line 53)
    C communication (line 55)
    D slightest   (line 57)

39 The writer concedes that public performances

    A are an introduction to poetry for some people.
    B may lead some people to acquire a taste for more serious poetry.
    C can be instructive as regards public speaking.
    D can be a good supplement to serious, written poetry.

40 In the text as a whole, the writer's purpose is to

    A foster greater unity among poets.
    B give advice to would-be poets.
    C persuade us of the value of poetry recitals.
    D analyse a current debate in the world of poetry.

PAPER 2   WRITING (2 hours)

Part 1

You **must** answer this question. Write your answer in **300–350** words in an appropriate style.

---

1 Your local council is proposing to ban all cars from the town centre because of problems with traffic, pollution and accidents. However, the following comments were made at a public meeting to discuss the situation:

> *My car is the only way I have of taking my children to school safely and quickly.*

> *The shops in the town centre will close because people will go elsewhere to do their shopping.*

> *Public transport here is dreadful. We can't rely on it and it is too expensive.*

The local council is inviting people to send in proposals in which they express their views on the council's plan and offer possible solutions to people's concerns.

Write your **proposal**.

Part 2

Write an answer to **one** of the questions **2–5** in this part. Write your answer in **300–350** words in an appropriate style.

---

2   A magazine has asked its readers to contribute to a series of articles called 'Things I want to achieve in the next ten years'. Readers are invited to submit articles in which they describe the achievements they feel are most important, and to give reasons for their choice. The article should make other readers think about the most important things in life.
Write your **article**.

3   The 'Family Page' in your local newspaper has invited readers to write in with descriptions of how they learnt the value of money when they were children. You decide to write a letter describing how as a child you came to appreciate the value of money, and how important money is to you now in relation to other things in your life.
Write your **letter**. Do not write any postal addresses.

4   The local history society you belong to produces a magazine whose purpose is to promote an appreciation of the past and the value of studying history. You have been asked to write a contribution for the magazine. You decide to write a report of a visit you have made to an historical building or site, pointing out how such visits can encourage the study of history.
Write your **report**.

5   Based on your reading of **one** of these books, write on **one** of the following.

(a) Anne Tyler: *The Accidental Tourist*
An arts magazine is planning a series on 'The Family in Twentieth Century Literature'. It has invited readers to send in a review of a book in which relationships between brothers and sisters play an important part. You decide to send in a review of *The Accidental Tourist*. You should focus on Macon's relationship with his brother and sister, and how and why this relationship changes during the novel.
Write your **review**.

(b) John Wyndham: *The Day of the Triffids*
A popular science magazine has invited articles on the theme of survival after major disasters. You send in an article based on your reading of *The Day of the Triffids*, outlining the events in the story and discussing how the survivors deal with their situation.
Write your **article**.

(c) Graham Greene: *Our Man in Havana*
You read the following opinion in a literary magazine:

'Now that International Relations have improved, spy novels have become an outdated and uninteresting literary form.'

You disagree and believe that *Our Man in Havana* is more than just a spy story. Write a letter to the magazine, making reference to the events, characters and relationships described in the book.

Write your **letter**. Do not write any postal addresses.

PAPER 3   USE OF ENGLISH (1 hour 30 minutes)

Part 1

For questions **1–15**, read the text below and think of the word which best fits each space. Use only **one** word in each space. There is an example at the beginning **(0)**.

Write your answers in CAPITAL LETTERS **on the separate answer sheet**.

Example: | 0 | T | H | E | S | E | | | | | | | | | | | | | | |

CAN PARROTS COMMUNICATE?

Everyone knows that parrots can imitate human speech, but can **(0)** ..*these*.. birds also understand meaning? Two decades ago, researcher Irene Pepperberg started working with Alex, an African grey parrot, and ever since then, she has been building **(1)** .... data on him. Pepperberg, **(2)** .... recently published book *The Alex Studies* makes fascinating reading, claims Alex doesn't copy speech but intentionally uses words to get **(3)** .... it is that he wants.

In actual **(4)** ...., some of his cognitive skills are identical to those of a five-year-old child. **(5)** .... a child's, Alex's learning has been a steady progression. Early on, he **(6)** .... vocalise whether two things were the same or different. Now, he carries **(7)** .... more complex tasks. Presented **(8)** .... different-coloured balls and blocks and asked the number of red blocks, he'll answer correctly. He requests things as well. **(9)** .... he ask to sit on your shoulder and you put him **(10)** .... else, he'll complain: 'Wanna go *shoulder*.'

A **(11)** .... experts remain sceptical, seeing very **(12)** .... in Alex's performance beyond learning by association, by **(13)** .... of intensive training. Yet Alex appears to **(14)** .... mastered simple two-way communication. As parrots live for 60 years or more, Alex may surprise **(15)** .... all further.

Part 2

For questions **16–25**, read the text below. Use the word given in capitals at the end of some of the lines to form a word that fits in the space in the same line. There is an example at the beginning **(0)**.

Write your answers in CAPITAL LETTERS **on the separate answer sheet**.

Example:

0	F	L	A	V	O	U	R	I	N	G								

VANILLA

Thanks to the ubiquitous use of vanilla as a **(0)** flavouring. in ice creams **FLAVOUR**
and cakes the world over, its taste is more **(16)** .... to the majority of **RECOGNISE**
people than the appearance of the plant.

The plant itself is actually a native of the tropical forests of Central America
and is the only variety of orchid to be grown on a commercial scale. Its delicate
white flowers open in the early morning and, after pollination by insects or
humming birds, a narrow bean-like pod forms and **(17)** .... , taking a **RIPE**
period of five to seven months to reach **(18)** .... It is this pod which is **MATURE**
harvested to provide the food crop we know as vanilla.

Despite its American origins, for decades it was only cultivated **(19)** .... **EXTEND**
on the Indian Ocean island of Madagascar, where it was introduced at the end
of the nineteenth century. It soon became clear that the vanilla grown there
was of a quality **(20)** .... in other areas, and the island quickly became **KNOW**
one of the world's major **(21)** .... **SUPPLY**

In recent years, however, new **(22)** .... have entered the vanilla market **COMPETE**
and, **(23)** .... , Madagascar's importance has started to slip. Of course, **CONSEQUENCE**
the **(24)** .... of new producers means a smaller market share, whilst the **EMERGE**
development of artificial substitutes is **(25)** .... to undermine demand for **THREAT**
the real thing.

Part 3

For questions **26–31**, think of **one** word only which can be used appropriately in all three sentences. Here is an example **(0)**.

Example:

0 Some of the tourists are hoping to get compensation for the poor state of the hotel, and I think they have a very .... case.

There's no point in trying to wade across the river, the current is far too ....

If you're asking me which of the candidates should get the job, I'm afraid I don't have any .... views either way.

0	S	T	R	O	N	G														

Write **only** the missing word in CAPITAL LETTERS **on the separate answer sheet**.

---

26 The prize-winning sculpture is on .... at the National Gallery this week.

As we rounded the bend, the first few houses came into ....

There is a widespread .... that too much sugar is bad for you.

27 We need to give some .... consideration to the downturn in our sales, and come up with a new marketing strategy.

The economic situation is so .... that the government has been forced to raise taxes.

He seems a real joker, but there's a more .... side to him, you know.

28 Francesca and Kate both .... a strong resemblance to their brother.

Life is too short to .... a grudge against your critics.

Once you reach the crossroads, ... left, and after that it's the second turning on the right.

29   The police officer warned the boys to keep .... of trouble.

Sophie isn't at all .... about her plans for the future.

From this viewpoint you can see the Rif Mountains on a .... day.

30   Jane left the engine .... while she delivered the parcel.

I'm surprised to hear the Governor of California is .... for President.

I've had that tune .... through my head ever since I heard it last week.

31   The team did so .... in the heats that they did not even reach the quarter-finals.

Some of our trees were .... damaged in the storm.

Their roof has been leaking for some time and is .... in need of repair.

Part 4

For questions **32–39**, complete the second sentence so that it has a similar meaning to the first sentence, using the word given. **Do not change the word given**. You must use between **three** and **eight** words, including the word given.

Here is an example **(0)**.

Example:

0 Do you mind if I watch you while you paint?

objection

Do you .... you while you paint?

0	*have any objection to my watching*

Write **only** the missing words **on the separate answer sheet**.

---

32 The author describes his childhood vividly in the book.

account

The author's book .... his childhood.

33 This plant often gets attacked by insects.

prone

This plant .... by insects.

34 Do you have any idea about how Jack made enough money to buy that new sports car?

light

Can you .... Jack made enough money to buy that new sports car?

35 Kate has finally accepted that their friendship is over.

terms

Kate has finally .... their friendship is over.

36 I wasn't expecting you to begin singing when they asked you to speak.

took

It .... singing when they asked you to speak.

37 Janice soon recovered from her cold.

get

It did .... her cold.

38 Only when the storm subsided was it clear just how much damage had been done.

extent

It was not .... of the damage was clear.

39 When he won the scholarship, Alan began to realise just how lucky he was.

dawn

When he won the scholarship, it began .... just how lucky he was.

Part 5

For questions **40–44**, read the following texts about art. For questions **40–43**, answer with a word or short phrase. You do not need to write complete sentences. For question **44**, write a summary according to the instructions given.

Write your answers to questions **40–44 on the separate answer sheet**.

A critic may crush an artist by telling him that what he has just done may be quite good in its own way, only it is not 'Art'. And that same critic may confound anyone enjoying a picture by declaring that what he liked in it was not the Art but something different.

Actually, I do not think there are wrong reasons for liking a statue or picture. Someone may like a landscape painting because it reminds him of home, or a portrait because it reminds him of a friend. There is nothing wrong with that. All of us, when we see a painting, are bound to be reminded of a hundred and one things which influence our likes and dislikes. As long as these memories help us to enjoy what we see, we need not worry. It is only when some irrelevant memory makes us   **line 10** prejudiced, when we instinctively turn away from a magnificent picture of an alpine scene because we dislike climbing, that we should search our mind for the reason for the aversion which spoils a pleasure we might otherwise have had. There *are* wrong reasons for disliking a work of art.

Most people like to see in pictures what they would also like to see in reality. This is quite a natural preference. We all like beauty in nature, and are grateful to the artists who have preserved it in their works.

40 In your own words, explain how, according to the writer, a viewer might react to a critic's comments about a work of art.

 ....

41 Explain what the writer means by 'some irrelevant memory makes us prejudiced' (lines 10–11).

 ....

Art has changed over the last few decades. Although continual change is the very essence of art, the most recent changes run far more deeply, and go beyond external appearances. The very concept of art is in fact being questioned. At first glance it might indeed seem to be mainly a matter of ephemeral and non-essential questions. For instance, contemporary art has never before enjoyed such wide popularity. Prices are soaring, and private   **line 6** collectors are currently placing an unprecedented number of orders. The prices for modern classics at auctions in London and New York have reached unimaginable heights, as art is increasingly regarded as a sound investment for the future.

Contemporary art has in fact become an integral part of today's middle-class society. Even works of art which are fresh from the studio are met with enthusiasm. They receive recognition rather quickly – too quickly for the taste of the surlier culture critics. Of course, not all works of art are bought immediately, but there is undoubtedly an increasing number of people who enjoy buying brand new works of art. Instead of fast and expensive cars, they buy the paintings, sculptures and photographic works of young artists. They know that contemporary art also adds to their social prestige. Furthermore, since art is not exposed to the same wear and tear as automobiles, it is – in principle – a far better investment.

42   Explain in your own words the evidence given by the writer of the 'wide popularity' (line 6) of art today.

....

43   Which phrase suggests new works of art are not always received positively when first displayed?

....

44   In a paragraph of between **50** and **70** words, summarise **in your own words as far as possible** the reasons given in the texts for why the public appreciate art. Write your summary **on the separate answer sheet**.

PAPER 4   LISTENING (40 minutes approximately)

Part 1

You will hear four different extracts. For questions **1–8**, choose the answer (**A**, **B** or **C**) which fits best according to what you hear. There are two questions for each extract.

Extract 1

You hear part of a discussion about a composer who writes film music.

1 The speaker particularly valued Nunan's earlier film music because

    A it portrayed suffering so well.
    B it was so passionate.
    C it gave insight to the film.

        1

2 How does the speaker feel about Nunan's current work?

    A cynical
    B angry
    C confused

        2

Extract 2

You hear part of an interview with an expert on human behaviour.

3 What does the expert's work involve?

    A transferring standard techniques from one field to another
    B persuading store employees to help in collecting data
    C interviewing customers in stores

        3

4 According to the expert's explanation, what is the purpose of a 'tracker'?

    A to interview customers for market research
    B to gather information unobtrusively
    C to influence people's buying behaviour

        4

Extract 3

You hear part of a radio programme in which a financial expert is asked about investing money in stocks and shares.

5 What is the expert doing when he speaks?

    A warning against specific investments

    B suggesting several courses of action

    C comparing investment techniques

6 According to the expert, what might make one investor more successful than the others?

    A having in-depth knowledge of a subject

    B benefiting from previous investment experience

    C investing in a wide range of companies

Extract 4

You hear the beginning of a radio interview with Irene Donovan, who leads an all-woman band.

7 Irene mentions the people who approach her because she wants to point out that

    A her band is the only one of its type.

    B there are several all-woman bands with her name.

    C she leads the best known all-woman band.

8 How did other band leaders react when Irene started her band?

    A They expected it to last only a short time.

    B They were worried about the competition from her band.

    C They were surprised there were enough woman musicians.

Part 2

You will hear part of a radio programme about chocolate. For questions **9–17**, complete the sentences with a word or short phrase.

Chocolate was originally regarded as a [   ] **9** food.

The [   ] **10** of chocolate is what makes us crave it.

During the manufacturing process the liquid chocolate is made smoother by passing it through [   ] **11**

In order to achieve an enjoyable [   ] **12** a thick emulsion is necessary.

According to Professor Warburton, some people may eat too much chocolate as a kind of [   ] **13**

A certain constituent of chocolate is known to increase [   ] **14** and blood sugar.

Eating chocolate may be one way of controlling [   ] **15** after something upsetting happens.

Stress hormones are produced as a result of a feeling of [   ] **16**

Corinne Sweet says people become addicted to chocolate because they have a [   ] **17**

Part 3

You will hear an interview with Derek Allen, an author, about the writing process. For questions **18–22**, choose the answer (**A**, **B**, **C** or **D**) which fits best according to what you hear.

18 Derek Allen thought his book would be successful because

    A it deals with an unusual subject.
    B he did a lot of research for it.
    C its packaging was appealing.
    D he invested a lot of effort in it.

| | 18 |

19 Allen says that writing for radio is useful because it

    A can be good preparation for writing a book.
    B makes you popular with a wide audience.
    C requires the same dialogue as a book.
    D allows you to introduce a variety of characters.

| | 19 |

20 Allen says he uses science fiction because

    A it represents his vision of what the future will be like.
    B many events can happen in a short space of time.
    C he wants to make it popular among readers.
    D it allows him to explore a bizarre chain of events.

| | 20 |

21 According to Allen, other writers use coincidence to

    A throw light on characters.
    B resolve difficulties with storylines.
    C make the reader work harder.
    D introduce an element of danger.

| | 21 |

22 If Allen was a painter, which element of a painting would he get wrong?

    A the background
    B the shape of the figures
    C the proportions
    D the detail

| | 22 |

Part 4

You will hear two travel agents talking about the rise in popularity of adventure holidays. For questions **23–28**, decide whether the opinions are expressed by only one of the speakers, or whether the speakers agree.

Write   **D**   for Daniel
        H   for Helena
or   **B**   for Both, where they agree.

___

23   Those who try adventure holidays soon find themselves addicted. | | **23** |

24   Adventure travellers are seeking an escape from their monotonous lives. | | **24** |

25   It seems as if adventure holidays would be a drain on your energy. | | **25** |

26   The thrill of adventure travel lies in being trapped in frightening situations. | | **26** |

27   People expect more from travel than their parents did. | | **27** |

28   A will to learn is the most important prerequisite for adventure travel. | | **28** |

PAPER 5 SPEAKING (19 minutes)

There are two examiners. One (the Interlocutor) conducts the test, providing you with the necessary materials and explaining what you have to do. The other examiner (the Assessor) will be introduced to you, but then takes no further part in the interaction.

Part 1 (3 minutes)

The Interlocutor first asks you and your partner a few questions which focus on information about yourselves and personal opinions.

Part 2 (4 minutes)

In this part of the test you and your partner are asked to talk together. The Interlocutor places a set of pictures on the table in front of you. This stimulus provides the basis for a discussion. The Interlocutor first asks an introductory question which focuses on one or two of the pictures. After about a minute, the Interlocutor gives you both a decision-making task based on the same set of pictures.

The pictures for Part 2 are on pages C2–C3 of the colour section.

Part 3 (12 minutes)

You are each given the opportunity to talk for two minutes, to comment after your partner has spoken and to take part in a more general discussion.

The Interlocutor gives you a card with a question written on it and asks you to talk about it for two minutes. After you have spoken, your partner is first asked to comment and then the Interlocutor asks you both another question related to the topic on the card. This procedure is repeated, so that your partner receives a card and speaks for two minutes, you are given an opportunity to comment and a follow-up question is asked.

Finally, the Interlocutor asks some further questions, which leads to a discussion on a general theme related to the subjects already covered in Part 3.

The cards for Part 3 are on pages C10–C11 of the colour section.

Test 2

PAPER 1   READING (1 hour 30 minutes)

Part 1

For questions **1–18**, read the three texts below and decide which answer (**A, B, C** or **D**) best fits each gap.

Mark your answers **on the separate answer sheet**.

Language

You and I belong to a species with a remarkable ability; we can shape events in each other's brains with exquisite precision. Language is so **(1)** .... woven into human experience that it is scarcely possible to imagine life without it. **(2)** .... are that if you find two or more people together anywhere on earth, they will soon be **(3)** .... words. When there is no one to talk with, people talk to themselves, to their dogs, even to their plants. I like to describe the skill of language as an 'instinct'. This **(4)** .... the idea that people know how to talk in more or less the sense that spiders know how to spin webs. Web-spinning was not invented by some unsung spider genius, and does not **(5)** .... having had the right education or on having an **(6)** .... for architecture or the construction trades.

1	A	rigidly	B	tightly	C	stiffly	D	tautly
2	A	Chances	B	Probabilities	C	Reasons	D	Explanations
3	A	sharing	B	reciprocating	C	exchanging	D	trading
4	A	transmits	B	disseminates	C	transfers	D	conveys
5	A	build on	B	depend on	C	count on	D	bank on
6	A	aptitude	B	applicability	C	intuition	D	intelligence

Climate and Weather

Climate and weather, which are mainly created by the air around us, profoundly affect the lives and distribution of animals and plants. Climate can be a dominating force on the character of landscapes. For example, warmth and wetness all the year round allow the growth of tropical jungles, which are natural **(7)** .... troves, with an incredible diversity of species. **(8)** .... cold, windswept areas can muster only a scattered selection of living things. The daily weather patterns that **(9)** .... up in the long term to the climate are caused by great masses of air rising and mixing, for the atmosphere is never still. Some of the motion is **(10)** .... the fact that the envelope of gases rests on a spinning globe; because air is thin it is not dragged along at the same speed as the earth, but tends to **(11)** .... behind. A more important **(12)** .... of turbulence, or air movement, however, is the sun.

7	**A**	prize	**B**	treasure	**C**	fortune	**D**	trophy
8	**A**	Subsequently	**B**	Conversely	**C**	Simultaneously	**D**	Eventually
9	**A**	make	**B**	join	**C**	add	**D**	load
10	**A**	along with	**B**	apart from	**C**	due to	**D**	given that
11	**A**	lag	**B**	stray	**C**	delay	**D**	linger
12	**A**	root	**B**	spring	**C**	font	**D**	source

Coffee

My duties as bar-person included serving drinks but, more worryingly, I was to be responsible for making coffee. In Lygon Street, Melbourne, a restaurant can stand or fall on its coffee reputation. There followed several days of intensive coffee-making training, in which I **(13)** .... more than I could ever wish to know about the cleaning and **(14)** .... of the restaurant's gleaming espresso machine. I learnt, too, about the essential principles **(15)** .... in making the perfect cup of rich, frothy cappuccino. By the end of the first week I had to admit that making a decent cup of coffee was not as easy as it looked and I **(16)** .... expected to be **(17)** .... to lowly ash-tray wiping duties again. Luckily, my boss was a patient man. 'Making coffee is both an art and a science,' he said, 'and you need time to **(18)** .... the knack.'

13	**A**	took in	**B**	carried off	**C**	pulled through	**D**	looked up
14	**A**	catering	**B**	service	**C**	preservation	**D**	maintenance
15	**A**	concerned	**B**	involved	**C**	needed	**D**	established
16	**A**	fully	**B**	wholly	**C**	mainly	**D**	nearly
17	**A**	banished	**B**	deported	**C**	punished	**D**	ordered
18	**A**	achieve	**B**	attain	**C**	activate	**D**	acquire

Part 2

You are going to read four extracts which are all concerned in some way with the notion of heritage. For questions **19–26**, choose the answer (**A**, **B**, **C** or **D**) which you think fits best according to the text.

Mark your answers **on the separate answer sheet**.

Heritage

The true meaning and significance of heritage is that it gives people and communities a genuine sense of connection with the past. Obviously, we feel connected to our personal heritage – usually, we know who and what our grandparents were, and we will have heard stories about how they lived. But, beyond that, there is a wider basic need to learn about our past, in order to help us understand and interpret our individual and national futures. Heritage represents a fundamental desire for continuity – assurance about the past goes a long way to assuring our future. It is through this continuity that we achieve our own place in history, our own 'immortality'.

In the same way that you inherit your genes, you also inherit a culture which has been passed down through many generations. There are aspects of your national heritage that you may not like or condone, but it is yours, and it is reassuring to feel a part of something.

Heritage has a phenomenal amount to teach us and, I would say, is imperative for our well-being. It affects everything from customs to material culture. Traditionally, our link with the past was through the stories and legends passed down by our ancestors. But, because Western industrial society broke up communities and families, much of that oral tradition has already been lost. Instead, places and architectural 'memories' give us clues to our past. It is vitally important to conserve and restore these links as a testament to our ancestors' identity.

19 How can the writer's argument in the first paragraph best be summarised?

   A Heritage can reveal a lot about what might happen to us.
   B Heritage can teach us a lot about how our grandparents lived.
   C Heritage enables us all to feel important and famous.
   D Heritage makes us wish for stability and security.

20 The writer's main intention is to

   A supply information.
   B give a definition.
   C suggest an approach.
   D encourage research.

The Fens

Some while ago I began a novel, *Waterland*, in which, though I did not know it then, the landscape of that part of England known as the Fens was to play a major part. Since the novel was published I have often been asked why, as an ignorant and perhaps presumptuous Londoner, I chose to write about a part of the country with which I have no personal connection. The short answer is that I chose the Fens because of their apparent unobtrusiveness – a flat and empty stage on which to set the drama of my book. This, as I learnt, was merely theory. The Fens, once one's imagination has got to grips with them, are neither flat nor empty. What I discovered was that the Fens, while as richly English as any other part of England, are also compellingly and hauntingly strange. It is remarkable that there should still exist in the middle of England a region which most English people find peculiarly foreign, especially when so many other distinctive (and remoter) areas of Britain have been ingested into the nation's cultural and literary heritage. The Fens are both empty and brimming, both cultivated and tenaciously wild, apparently 'open' and 'obvious' yet profoundly mysterious.

My own physical researches while writing my novel were in fact not so extensive. I have never been, yet, to Wisbech or Prickwillow. As a writer of fiction I am interested in imagined worlds, and I would much rather hazard an inspired guess at some point of authenticity than go for documentary proof. Yet this very attempt to 'imagine' the Fens has its special logic, for, as the pages of Edward Storey's scholarly book abundantly show, the Fens are, peculiarly, not just a landscape but a state of mind.

21 What does the writer come to realise about the Fens?

    A   He underestimated the area at first.
    B   He needed a more inspiring setting for his novel.
    C   He should have done more research about the area.
    D   He was wrong to think of the area as typically English.

22 What distinction can be made between the writer and Edward Storey?

    A   Storey has a greater eye for detail.
    B   Storey is the more rational writer.
    C   Their books serve different purposes.
    D   They interpret the Fens in opposite ways.

Museums

Museums must make their collections accessible. In the past, this simply meant packing them into display cases, often with wordy labels that made little concession to the lay person. Nowadays, accessibility should demand more than this. Displays can be lively and interesting, making the best use of theatrical or architectural techniques to capture visitors' attention and perhaps stimulate emotional response. But museums should be about more than their displays. They should make their collections accessible to the widest possible community. The provision of loan boxes of objects for class teachers is one known example of this and, recently, this principle has been extended by some museums so that similar material is made available for use in treating elderly people who are losing their memory.

Museums concern themselves with 'artefacts and specimens' – not replicas. They exist to facilitate an encounter with authenticity. They present items that actually existed – were used – had meaning – at some historical time. This is their great strength, and is what distinguishes them from heritage centres and theme parks, books and CD-ROMs. Museums which rise to the challenge which this distinction implies and provide exciting and accessible displays, catalogues and outreach programmes, will find that their apparent competitors in 'virtual history' are in fact their allies, stimulating an appetite for the 'real thing' that museums are uniquely placed to satisfy.

23 The advantage of today's museums over older museums is that

    A   they draw on resources in the community.
    B   they are more affordable for the non-expert.
    C   they go beyond the merely visual.
    D   they have more space for their collections.

24 In the second paragraph, the writer implies that museums

    A   are failing to keep pace with changing technology.
    B   need to realise that their future lies in their own efforts.
    C   may have been too competitive in the past.
    D   are too preoccupied with the notion of authenticity.

Architecture and Environment

The desire to preserve things is not new, but now change in our towns comes with such speed and on such a scale that most of us are affected by it in some way. It turns some people into rabid preservationists and it encourages others to think more closely about the nature of towns as we know them today and their future.

It may be quite reasonably argued that the generations who have lived through events such as world wars and the like are more inclined to preservation than their predecessors – anything which expresses stability becomes important. If there is a psychological need for preservation it is part of the planner's job to take account of it.

Change is no enemy if we learn how to handle it. Physical change, in other words, change in the environment provided by our towns, reflects social change – change in our numbers, in our welfare and in our demands.

25 What is the writer's view of change?

    A   It can be managed effectively.
    B   It is a consequence of catastrophe.
    C   It is a psychological necessity.
    D   It should be avoided if possible.

26 In this passage, the writer is

    A   analysing a problem.
    B   outlining his position.
    C   presenting his objections.
    D   rejecting opposing views.

Part 3

You are going to read an extract from a novel. Seven paragraphs have been removed from the extract. Choose from the paragraphs **A–H** the one which fits each gap (**27–33**). There is one extra paragraph which you do not need to use.

Mark your answers **on the separate answer sheet**.

The two sisters kept Lily's driving a secret from Chen for some time. She would drive around the allotments and the railway line and gasworks, shooting the tiny hump-backed bridge with all four wheels in the air and a tremendous bump (Lily's only misjudgement), before completing the journey by the gasworks in an odour of sulphur and brimstone. Chen, however, was actually amused by what his wife had been doing behind his back. 'So you can really drive it then, Lily? Well done!'

27	

They fixed on a Monday at the beginning of next month. This was the slackest day of the week; they decided to leave early in the morning and return by midday. That way they need lose no customers. In the meantime Lily would practise around the allotments.

28	

Within an hour of stepping over the newspapers and out of the front door, they were looking at the English Channel. Lily had driven impeccably. Even Mui, sitting in the back ready to give directions, one hand on the cross-braces of Man Kee's rompers as he pressed his nose against the window, had to grant this. On the road Lily had actually overtaken a couple of laggard vehicles with immense verve and such timing that Mui had pressed her lips closely together against her own protest. <u>Chen</u> went as far as applauding.

29	

She was unclear about the meanings of the various roadmarkings and preferred to pay a fee rather than risk being towed away. Or even being served with a summons. Might this evidence of basic prudence set Mui's mind at rest? On the way down Lily had several times observed her elder sister's taut face in the driving mirror, which she used with great frequency. Perhaps it would be best not to put worries in Mui's mind which would not have occurred to her in the first place. Lily personally locked all the van doors and meticulously tested each in turn.

30	

Taken aback, Chen took Man Kee ahead of the two sisters to look at the grey barbarian sea. He perched Son on the top railing and put his arms around his stomach. Man Kee was a soft, warm, and what was more, these days an increasingly responsive bundle. He reacted by putting his hand, a tiny replica of the shape of Chen's, with its broad palm and stubby fingers, on his father's sleeve.

31	

There was a trail of smoke just before the horizon met the sea in a thin line and then, suddenly shimmering in the glitter of the rising morning sun on the metal waves, a hull; and in a small curve of the railings was a grey telescope. The sparkle of the water instantly altered Chen's mood.

32	

33	

Chen lifted Man Kee to the eyepiece. 'Do you see the ship, Son?' he asked softly. 'It is a special little ship for people like us, Son. It is very little and very old but that is only what strangers see. We know better, don't we, Son, because it is the ship that will take us all back home when we are finished here. It will take you to your homeland, Son, which you have never seen.'

Man Kee would not be parted from the telescope and when he had been persuaded to relinquish his grip the whirring inside the mounting had stopped and all Lily could see was a quivering opaque circle of white light with a scratched surface. By the time Chen had found a second coin the ship was over the horizon and Lily was left with a view of seagulls scavenging gash in the wake.

A He put a coin in the slot and trained the glass on the ship. He was unable to find it at first, although he had aimed off carefully with the gun-sight on top of the barrel. Chen swung the tube in wide circles. There it was! Gone again. Chen swivelled the instrument more carefully. Now he had it in the centre of the circle, surprisingly large, red, and very rusty with a small bow wave: tramp steamer.

B They went along the promenade. There was an amusement arcade, built into the cliff. They stared at the rows of fruit machines, the gauntlet of pin-ball tables. Chen was fumbling in his pocket when Lily gave him a coin.

C Men were strange creatures, Mui thought. Brother-in-law should have been upset about this. Yet he was soon enthusiastically making plans with Lily for a jaunt and obviously revelling in her mastery of this new skill.

D And it was in that moment that Chen resolved to bring Son up *his* way. He would have an education in figures (Chen's own weak point) and grow up to own many restaurants, gaining experience in all aspects of the trade on the way. The sombre sea put Chen in a pleasing melancholy as he planned Man Kee's career.

E Now, after coming through the gasworks of this seaside town (reassuring, familiar sight), past the lagoon and its miniature motor boats, they were moving smoothly along the empty promenade. Lily parked in a small street off the sea front which was full of empty bays.

F Chen kissed the top of Man Kee's head. Behind him now were Lily and Mui. Lily put her arm round Husband's shoulders. 'The little old ship,' said Chen. 'Let your mother see, Son.'

G 'Don't worry,' Chen joked. 'No one will want that heap of tin.' The girls bristled. Lily accused her husband of ingratitude. Mui rebuked him for being proud and too readily deceived by appearances.

H Resolved to go along with the majority despite her personal misgivings, Mui had been to buy a road-map. She had been able to get a ten percent discount, which impressed Chen, though Lily felt a bit insulted by Mui's lack of faith in her navigating abilities.

Part 4

You are going to read an extract from a novel. For questions **34–40**, choose the answer (**A, B, C** or **D**) which you think fits best according to the text.

Mark your answers **on the separate answer sheet**.

I have never begun a novel with more misgiving. If I call it a novel it is only because I don't know what else to call it. I have little story to tell and I end neither with a death or a marriage. Instead I leave my reader in the air. This book consists of my recollections of a man with whom I was thrown into close contact only at long intervals, and I have little knowledge of what happened to him in between. I suppose that by the exercise of invention I could fill the gaps plausibly enough and so make my narrative more coherent; but I have no wish to do that. I only want to set down what I know.

To save embarrassment to people still living I have given to the persons who play a part in this story names of my own contriving, and I have in other ways taken pains to make sure that no one should recognise them. The man I am writing about is not famous. It may be that he never will be. It may be that when his life at last comes to an end he will leave no more trace of his sojourn on earth than a stone thrown into a river leaves on the surface of the water. Then my book, if it is read at all, will be read only for what intrinsic interest it may possess. But it may be that the way of life that he has chosen for himself and the peculiar strength and sweetness of his character may have an ever-growing influence over his fellow men so that, long after his death perhaps, it may be realised that there lived in this age a very remarkable creature. Then it will be quite clear of whom I write in this book and those who want to know at least a little about his early life may find in it something to their purpose. I think my book, within its acknowledged limitations, will be a useful source of information to my friend's biographers.

I do not pretend that the conversations I have recorded can be regarded as verbatim reports. I never kept notes of what was said on this or the other occasions, but I have a good memory for what concerns me, and though I have put these conversations in my own words they faithfully represent, I believe, what was said. I remarked a little while back that I have invented nothing but I have taken the liberty that historians have taken to put into the mouths of the persons of my narrative speeches that I did not myself hear and could not possibly have heard. I have done this for the same reasons that the historians have, to give liveliness and verisimilitude to scenes that would have been ineffective if they had been merely recounted. I want to be read and I think I am justified in doing what I can to make my book readable. The intelligent reader will easily see for himself where I have used this artifice, and he is at perfect liberty to reject it.

Another reason that has caused me to embark upon this work with apprehension is that the persons I have chiefly to deal with are of another culture. It is very difficult to know people and I don't think one can ever really know any but one's own countrymen. For men and women are not only themselves; they are also the region in which they were born, the city apartment or the farm in which they learnt to walk, the games they played as children, the food they ate, the schools they attended, the sports they followed and the poets they read. It is all these things that have made them what they are, and these are the things that you can't come to know by hearsay, you can only know them if you have lived them. You can only know if you are them. And because you cannot know persons of a nation foreign to you except from observation, it is difficult to give them credibility in the pages of a book. I have never attempted to deal with any but my own countrymen, and if I have ventured to do otherwise in short stories it is because in them you can treat your characters more summarily. You give the reader broad indications and leave him to fill in the details. In this book, I do not pretend that my characters are as they would see themselves; they are seen, as is my main character, through my own eyes.

34   In the first paragraph, the author reveals that he

    A   is dissatisfied with the conclusion of his novel.
    B   has superficial understanding of his main character.
    C   has resisted employing certain literary techniques.
    D   is disapproving of mainstream fiction writing.

35   In discussing the identity of the characters in the novel, the author shows his

    A   respect for historical fact.
    B   sensitivity towards others.
    C   awareness of stylistic conventions.
    D   understanding of human relationships.

36   What does the author suggest about his main character in paragraph 2?

    A   His appeal to the reader is difficult to predict.
    B   The role he plays is likely to be controversial.
    C   The choices he makes are rather conventional.
    D   His approach to life reflects the era in which he lived.

37   In discussing the dialogue in the novel, the author states that it

    A   involves some distortion of the facts.
    B   contains some obvious literary embellishments.
    C   can be trusted to reflect the spirit of the age.
    D   has been re-worked to fit the style of the novel.

38   In the third paragraph, while expanding on his inventiveness as a writer, the author

    A   denies an influence on his work.
    B   supports an earlier statement that he made.
    C   corrects a false assumption about his style.
    D   defends the technique he has used in the novel.

39   The author's tone in discussing culture in the final paragraph is

    A   accusatory.
    B   embarrassed.
    C   explanatory.
    D   ambivalent.

40   In the extract, the writer makes it clear that this novel

    A   will benefit a certain type of reader.
    B   successfully combines fact and fiction.
    C   may contain some inaccurate claims.
    D   is untypical of his work in general.

PAPER 2   WRITING (2 hours)

Part 1

You **must** answer this question. Write your answer in **300–350** words in an appropriate style.

___

1 You have attended a course on 'Computing in the 21ˢᵗ Century' and have been asked by your tutor to write an essay on the future role of computers in education. You have been to a lecture on this subject and have made the notes below. You write your essay using your notes and expressing your own opinions.

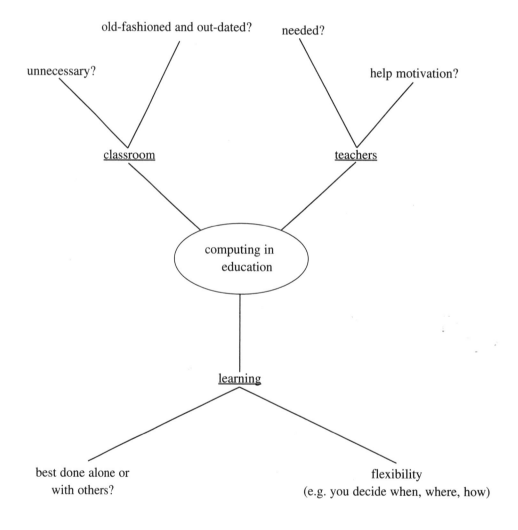

Write your **essay**.

Part 2

Write an answer to **one** of the questions **2–5** in this part. Write your answer in **300–350** words in an appropriate style.

---

2 Your college has been given funding to improve its leisure and sports facilities for students. The college principal has asked people to send in proposals on how the money can be best spent. In your proposal comment on the present facilities, and make recommendations for improving and extending them.
Write your **proposal**.

3 Your local tourist office has launched a competition to encourage people to eat out more often at local restaurants. To win the prize, a holiday weekend, you must write a review of a visit to a restaurant of your choice to celebrate a special occasion. Describe the interior, the food and the service, and say whether you would recommend the restaurant and why.
Write your **review**.

4 A radio programme is running a competition to find the 'Personality of the Decade'. Listeners wishing to nominate a personality are asked to write letters to the radio station giving details of the individual they have chosen and explaining why they think this person should win the title. The person should be well-known and should have made a significant contribution in their particular field during the past ten years.
Write your **letter**. Do not write any postal addresses.

5 Based on your reading of **one** of these books, write on **one** of the following.

(a) Anne Tyler: *The Accidental Tourist*
A series of articles has been looking at the treatment of unconventional lifestyles in modern literature. Readers have been asked to send in contributions. You write an article in which you describe the Leary household and compare it with Muriel's home in Singleton Street, and say how Macon adapts to each one.
Write your **article**.

(b) John Wyndham: *The Day of the Triffids*
The Editor of the Arts Page of a newspaper has asked for letters on what kind of books make good films. Write a letter saying why you think *The Day of the Triffids* would make a successful science fiction film, making particular reference to how different characters respond to fear of the unknown.
Write your **letter**. Do not write any postal addresses.

(c) Graham Greene: *Our Man in Havana*
A magazine is running a series of articles on likeable villains in English literature. You have recently read *Our Man in Havana* and decide to write an article for this series. In your article you should describe Captain Segura's character, and refer to the aspects of his behaviour and actions which led Mr Wormold to say of him 'he wasn't a bad chap'.
Write your **article**.

PAPER 3   USE OF ENGLISH (1 hour 30 minutes)

Part 1

For questions **1–15**, read the text below and think of the word which best fits each space. Use only **one** word in each space. There is an example at the beginning **(0)**.

Write your answers in CAPITAL LETTERS **on the separate answer sheet**.

Example:

```
0  H  A  S
```

GARDEN WILDLIFE

The age of a garden **(0)** .....*has*.... a great effect on the abundance of its wildlife. Since most animals depend ultimately on plants for their food, animal life cannot easily establish **(1)** .... in the absence of plant life. A plot of land behind a newly-built house, even **(2)** .... covered with a layer of good soil, will support very **(3)** .... resident species other **(4)** .... microscopic organisms. **(5)** .... from the odd worm or spider, not **(6)** .... creatures will be able to **(7)** .... a living in the garden **(8)** .... this stage.

Colonisation takes **(9)** .... gradually. Humans may introduce plants, and weed seeds will arrive on the breeze or be dropped by passing birds. Insects and other animals visit the garden and, given suitable conditions, they take **(10)** .... residence there. **(11)** .... all this activity, however, it takes years for a garden to become fully populated, and it cannot really be regarded as mature until it is **(12)** .... of supporting fully-grown shrubs and trees. On **(13)** .... basis, a large number of British gardens are immature, **(14)** .... as much as they do not support **(15)** .... a variety of wildlife as an older garden.

Part 2

For questions **16–25**, read the text below. Use the word given in capitals at the end of some of the lines to form a word that fits in the space in the same line. There is an example at the beginning **(0)**.

Write your answers in CAPITAL LETTERS **on the separate answer sheet**.

Example: | 0 | P | R | O | B | A | B | L | Y | | | | | | | | | | | |

LANGUAGE CHANGE

The phenomenon of language change **(0)** ..*probably*.. attracts more public notice **PROBABLE**

and more **(16)** .... than any other linguistic issue. There is a widely held **DISAPPROVE**

belief that change must mean deterioration and decay. Older people observe

the casual speech of the young and conclude that standards have fallen

(17) .... **APPRECIATE**

It is understandable that many people dislike change, but it is **(18)** .... to **WISE**

condemn all linguistic **(19)** .... It is often felt that contemporary language **MODIFY**

illustrates the problem at its worst, but this belief is shared by every generation.

There are indeed cases where linguistic change can lead to problems of

unintelligibility and **(20)** .... , and if change is too rapid there can be **AMBIGUOUS**

major communication problems. But as a rule, the parts of language which are

(21) .... change at any given time are relatively small in comparison to **GO**

the vast, unchanging areas of language. It is because change is so **(22)** .... **FREQUENT**

that it is so distinctive and **(23)** .... Some degree of caution and **NOTICE**

concern is therefore always desirable for the **(24)** .... of precision and **MAINTAIN**

(25) .... communication, but there are no grounds for the extremely **EFFECT**

pessimistic attitudes so often encountered.

Part 3

For questions **26–31**, think of **one** word only which can be used appropriately in all three sentences. Here is an example **(0)**.

Example:

0 Some of the tourists are hoping to get compensation for the poor state of the hotel, and I think they have a very .... case.

There's no point in trying to wade across the river, the current is far too ....

If you're asking me which of the candidates should get the job, I'm afraid I don't have any .... views either way.

0	S	T	R	O	N	G															

Write **only** the missing word in CAPITAL LETTERS **on the separate answer sheet**.

---

26 A key witness can often provide detailed corroboration, thus having a dramatic .... on the outcome of a complex legal case.

It's generally agreed that the .... of television in the modern world is considerable.

Martha Graham played a major role in developing the theory of modern dance, so extending her .... to a whole new generation of dancers.

27 My boss is extremely efficient, but unfortunately she's not always very .... to other people's worries.

In the play, James Collard gave a .... portrayal of the artist as a young man.

My brother was always an extremely .... child, and we had to be very careful what we said to him.

28 Paul Smith has always been totally .... to helping others less fortunate than himself.

Anna's absolutely .... to her career as a surgeon; nothing else is really important to her.

The singer George Andrew has .... several of his most recent songs to his wife.

29 Any new decisions the committee takes must be in .... with previous policy.

  If Simon is going to take that .... , I don't think he will persuade anyone.

  George reached the edge of the field and caught sight of a .... of trees in the distance.

30 Sarah felt great .... when she heard about the accident.

  The conference catering arrangements are not Mrs Robinson's ....

  The new printing company my uncle established is now a thriving ....

31 John has great .... in his mechanic's ability to get the car going.

  My father is usually successful in interviews owing to his air of ....

  Susan has never betrayed a .... and I don't think she ever will.

Part 4

For questions **32–39**, complete the second sentence so that it has a similar meaning to the first sentence, using the word given. **Do not change the word given**. You must use between **three** and **eight** words, including the word given.

Here is an example (**0**).

Example:

0 Do you mind if I watch you while you paint?

objection

Do you .... you while you paint?

0	have any objection to my watching

Write **only** the missing words **on the separate answer sheet**.

---

32 Only passengers with Gold Star tickets may use the executive lounge.

restricted

Use of the executive lounge ....
possession of Gold Star tickets.

33 You should not lock this door for any reason when the building is open to the public.

circumstances

Under .... locked when the building is
open to the public.

34 Helen was always embarrassed by her father's jokes.

source

Helen's father's jokes .... her.

35 How likely is the new venture to get off the ground?

prospects

What .... off the ground?

36 Damien paid little attention to his brother's warnings.

notice

Damien didn't .... his brother's
warnings.

37 In Colin's opinion, he hasn't done anything he should apologise for.

concerned

As .... , he hasn't done anything he
should apologise for.

38 Dr Potter was offended by some of the remarks that were made about her work.

exception

Dr Potter .... some of the remarks
that were made about her work.

39 She had her own reasons for not telling us anything about her past.

dark

As to her past, she kept us ....
reasons.

Part 5

For questions **40–44**, read the following texts about the constraints of modern life. For questions **40–43**, answer with a word or short phrase. You do not need to write complete sentences. For question **44**, write a summary according to the instructions given.

Write your answers to questions **40–44 on the separate answer sheet**.

Because man's original need to hunt in order to survive has all but disappeared, we are now free to replace it with whatever symbolic substitution takes our fancy, just so long as it contains some of the basic elements. Today, for most people, 'going to work' is the major substitute for hunting. For the lucky ones, the nature of their daily work is sufficiently close to the pattern of the primeval hunt to be satisfying. The executives who set off in the morning, eager to make a 'killing' in the city, with their schemes and strategies, their team tactics and targets, their immediate aims and long-term goals, hoping to confirm a contract or close a deal, and eventually to 'bring home the bacon', are the fulfilled pseudo-hunters of modern times. But for   **line 9** many other people, their work is so boringly repetitive that it provides little of the challenge of the hunt and is a poor substitute for it. If we were descendants of cud-chewing herbivores, this would not matter, but we are not. People whose work   **line 12** is boring become restless and frustrated. They have to find other outlets for their 'hunter's brain'. Some of these outlets are creative. Others can be highly destructive. For many individuals, a lack of 'job satisfaction', which can usually be traced to a lack of potential for symbolic hunting, is only made tolerable by the development of some kind of hobby or private passion.

40 Why is the phrase 'bring home the bacon' (line 9) particularly appropriate?

....

41 In your own words, explain why repetitive work would not be a problem for descendants of 'cud-chewing herbivores' (line 12).

....

Biologically, human beings are aroused by the amount of stimulation around them and the modern city is full of sights that trigger psychological arousal. When we walk through cities we are bombarded by stimuli of all types. Imagine walking into a busy street with the noise of people, cars and roadworks. The sounds may be unpleasant but still stimulate us. Adrenalin pumps through our body, making us react more quickly than normal; our heart rate increases the blood flow to our muscles, enabling us to break quickly into a run to catch a bus. Our heightened arousal means that we can react quickly.

Although this can be useful, there is a limit to how much our senses can take in at once. When we step off a train at a busy station after a relatively quiet journey, our senses are bombarded. There is simply too much noise and too much happening for our brain to process. We're overloaded. The general level of arousal in the busy station may enable us to attend to more of the stimuli, but we still have to ignore some of what is happening, as we do not have the capacity to deal with everything: it is as if we have tunnel vision.   **line 15**

City life consists of a huge number of encounters with potential sensory and information overload. The necessary filtering out of some of these stimuli has been **line 17** institutionalised into new rules of behaviour for the city. People don't stop and talk, they keep their faces blank and their eyes straight ahead. They are not just protecting themselves, but avoiding overloading others.

42   What does the writer mean by 'tunnel vision' (line 15)?

....

43   Explain why, according to the writer, it is necessary to filter out 'some of these stimuli' (line 17) in modern city life?

....

44   In a paragraph of between **50** and **70** words, summarise **in your own words as far as possible** how, according to the texts, human beings respond to life in modern society. Write your summary **on the separate answer sheet**.

PAPER 4   LISTENING (40 minutes approximately)

Part 1

You will hear four different extracts. For questions **1–8**, choose the answer (**A**, **B** or **C**) which fits best according to what you hear. There are two questions for each extract.

Extract 1

You hear part of a radio interview about an amusement park and its founder.

1 Why does Ray Taylor say he only goes on some rides once?

    A   to indicate how busy he is
    B   to show he has checked them all
    C   to make them seem exciting

1

2 Charles Wicksteed's job was

    A   running the park.
    B   managing an engineering company.
    C   inventing machines.

2

Extract 2

You hear a rock musician speaking about his early life.

3 What made the speaker, as a child, interested in his father's hobby?

    A   It seemed rather mysterious and scary.
    B   It was his only chance to listen to the radio.
    C   It opened the outside world up to him.

3

4 How did he feel when he first heard his record on the radio?

    A   overjoyed
    B   shocked
    C   embarrassed

4

You hear a radio announcement telling listeners about an arts programme later in the evening.

5 The subject of tonight's programme is

- **A** a new theatrical production.
- **B** actors in film and theatre.
- **C** the analysis of one type of play.

6 Rowntree has chosen a new area of work because

- **A** he enjoys theatre work so much.
- **B** he wants to have an overview of theatre.
- **C** he is getting too old to be a director.

Extract 4

You hear a speaker talking about a medicine called 'PROKAZ' and how she chose its name.

7 The speaker said she wanted to choose a name that

- **A** could be used in many different languages.
- **B** would suggest the qualities of the product.
- **C** would be easy to remember.

8 'KAZ' was chosen as part of the name 'PROKAZ' because

- **A** modern scientists used these letters.
- **B** it already existed.
- **C** it sounded progressive.

Part 2

You will hear the beginning of an interview in which a university professor talks about the robot he has designed, called Jeremy. For questions **9–17**, complete the sentences with a word or short phrase.

In the trials, Jeremy had to find his way round a complicated

| | 9 | without problems.

Professor Shepherd mentions

| | 10 | as a possibly dangerous substance that robots can deal with.

He believes that making robots will help researchers to understand

| | 11 | itself.

Researchers decided to use the model of ants, whose

| | 12 | are adequate for their needs.

In appearance, Jeremy most resembles a | | 13 | on wheels.

Jeremy has a | | 14 | attached on top of him.

Professor Shepherd compares giving Jeremy rewards and punishments with

| | 15 |

Professor Shepherd describes his use of the terms 'reward' and 'punishment' as a kind of

| | 16 |

He gives the example of a robotic

| | 17 | to show how far domestic robots have developed.

Part 3

You will hear an interview with Dr Janet Thompson, who spent many years in Africa observing chimpanzees. For questions **18–22**, choose the answer (**A**, **B**, **C** or **D**) which fits best according to what you hear.

---

18 When Dr Thompson first saw a chimpanzee using a blade of grass as a tool,

    A   it made her feel much closer to the animal.
    B   it confirmed one of her theories.
    C   it fulfilled her expectations.
    D   it had no initial impact on her.

> 18

19 Dr Thompson was not worried about her personal safety while in Africa because

    A   wild animals tend to avoid conflict with humans.
    B   she had never been hurt by an animal.
    C   the potentially dangerous chimpanzees knew her well.
    D   she was able to avoid the wild animals.

> 19

20 According to Dr Thompson, the only disadvantage of bringing up her son in Gombe was

    A   the lack of expert medical services in case of illness.
    B   the risk of drowning in the lake.
    C   the danger of attack by a wild animal.
    D   the fact that there were no other children of his age.

> 20

21 Dr Thompson corrects the interviewer by explaining that father chimpanzees

    A   are unlikely to take on a paternal role.
    B   keep male intruders or rivals at a distance.
    C   extend their territory for reasons of pride.
    D   rescue their females from danger.

> 21

22 Dr Thompson decided to leave Gombe and the chimpanzees because

    A   she wanted the company of people again.
    B   there was little more to be discovered about their habits.
    C   she felt impelled to tell people about the problem.
    D   her research needed to be taken to the next stage.

> 22

Part 4

You will hear two friends, Kathy and Derek, talking about films based on 19th century novels. For questions **23–28**, decide whether the opinions are expressed by only one of the speakers, or whether the speakers agree.

Write   **K**   for Kathy
       D   for Derek
or   **B**   for Both, where they agree.

---

23   In the film *Oliver Twist*, it was hard to think of the actors as the characters they were playing.   **23**

24   Film adaptations of the 1930s and 40s reflect their own time.   **24**

25   Film adaptations made nowadays may reflect current attitudes.   **25**

26   The actor sometimes does not match your idea of the character.   **26**

27   The author's viewpoint should be evident in film adaptations.   **27**

28   The film audience are able to reach their own conclusions about the characters.   **28**

PAPER 5   SPEAKING (19 minutes)

There are two examiners. One (the Interlocutor) conducts the test, providing you with the necessary materials and explaining what you have to do. The other examiner (the Assessor) will be introduced to you, but then takes no further part in the interaction.

Part 1 (3 minutes)

The Interlocutor first asks you and your partner a few questions which focus on information about yourselves and personal opinions.

Part 2 (4 minutes)

In this part of the test you and your partner are asked to talk together. The Interlocutor places a set of pictures on the table in front of you. This stimulus provides the basis for a discussion. The Interlocutor first asks an introductory question which focuses on one or two of the pictures. After about a minute, the Interlocutor gives you both a decision-making task based on the same set of pictures.

The pictures for Part 2 are on pages C4–C5 of the colour section.

Part 3 (12 minutes)

You are each given the opportunity to talk for two minutes, to comment after your partner has spoken and to take part in a more general discussion.

The Interlocutor gives you a card with a question written on it and asks you to talk about it for two minutes. After you have spoken, your partner is first asked to comment and then the Interlocutor asks you both another question related to the topic on the card. This procedure is repeated, so that your partner receives a card and speaks for two minutes, you are given an opportunity to comment and a follow-up question is asked.

Finally, the Interlocutor asks some further questions, which leads to a discussion on a general theme related to the subjects already covered in Part 3.

The cards for Part 3 are on pages C10–C11 of the colour section.

Test 3

PAPER 1 READING (1 hour 30 minutes)

Part 1

For questions **1–18**, read the three texts below and decide which answer (**A**, **B**, **C** or **D**) best fits each gap.

Mark your answers **on the separate answer sheet**.

Othello

The transfer to London from Stratford of an exceptional production of Shakespeare's play *Othello* allows me to make **(1)** .... for an unfair review that I wrote when the show opened last spring. Back then I complained that Ray Fearon was too young to play the title role and I was guilty of running down his acting. I still think it's a distortion of the tragedy to remove the age difference between Othello and Desdemona but I eat my **(2)** .... about the rest of Mr Fearon's magnificent performance. Indeed the whole cast is magnificent. Memorable scenes include the one where Cassio's competitive games with the other young officers get dangerously out of **(3)** .... , and the moment when Iago begins to lose control and has to struggle to get a **(4)** .... on himself. And I challenge anyone not to be **(5)** .... to tears during the scene where Emilia prepares Desdemona for bed. The **(6)** .... and tension throughout are terrific. Do not miss this production.

1	**A**	confessions	**B**	amends	**C**	compensation	**D**	recourse
2	**A**	thoughts	**B**	words	**C**	ideas	**D**	comments
3	**A**	turn	**B**	place	**C**	reach	**D**	hand
4	**A**	brake	**B**	grasp	**C**	rein	**D**	grip
5	**A**	drawn	**B**	sent	**C**	moved	**D**	carried
6	**A**	pace	**B**	dash	**C**	rate	**D**	haste

Lake Vostok

In the heart of Antarctica, nothing **(7)** .... . On the fringes of the continent there are penguins, seals and birds aplenty. But up on the great white plateau in the interior, life has no foothold. Except, **(8)** .... , in a vast hidden expanse of freshwater named Lake Vostok which lies beneath nearly

4 kilometres of ice, directly below the coldest **(9)** .... on earth. The water has been isolated from air and sunlight for up to 25 million years. Biologists can hardly wait to **(10)** .... its mysterious depths and discover what strange organisms lurk within. Geologists and glaciologists are hot on their **(11)** .... . For two years now, researchers round the world have been plotting ways to uncover the lake's secrets, and, if they get their wish, in the next few years we will **(12)** .... the decade of Lake Vostok.

7 A	stalks	**B**	stirs	**C**	suits	**D**	sounds
8 A	that is	**B**	for example	**C**	in effect	**D**	as such
9 A	tip	**B**	speck	**C**	spot	**D**	dot
10 A	burrow	**B**	plunge	**C**	tunnel	**D**	probe
11 A	heels	**B**	knees	**C**	paces	**D**	steps
12 A	present	**B**	witness	**C**	expose	**D**	reveal

Scientists

There was an interesting thing on the radio last week. It seems that a bunch of scientists are getting themselves hot under the **(13)** .... over what drives them to be scientists; the expression 'because it's there' **(14)** .... to mind. Sure we all know it's the age-old **(15)** .... for knowledge, the desire to understand everything from the atom to the black hole. But what these guys want to know is why we want to know all of this in the first **(16)** .... and why can't science explain why we want to know?

Surely, it's more important to know whether what we scientists are doing is right, rather than get **(17)** .... in debates over the point of it all. I would have thought that the crucial issue here is not why we pursue it, but to **(18)** .... that science is a tool, and we are the ones who should decide how, where, when and why to use it.

13 A	shirt	**B**	collar	**C**	cuff	**D**	hat
14 A	trips	**B**	bounds	**C**	springs	**D**	slips
15 A	mission	**B**	quest	**C**	journey	**D**	expedition
16 A	place	**B**	stage	**C**	step	**D**	part
17 A	pulled up	**B**	dragged up	**C**	slowed down	**D**	bogged down
18 A	identify	**B**	accommodate	**C**	distinguish	**D**	recognise

Part 2

You are going to read four extracts which are all concerned in some way with people and places. For questions **19–26**, choose the answer (**A**, **B**, **C** or **D**) which you think fits best according to the text.

Mark your answers **on the separate answer sheet**.

Philadelphia Avenue

I headed down Philadelphia Avenue on the odd-numbered side. The dusk had deepened, the humidity thickened into a palpable, prickly drizzle that lent my walk a heightened feeling of sheltered stealth. I knew this side of the street from the dawn of consciousness; our neighbours the Matzes and the Pritchards, and Han Kieffer's grocery store, and the Krings' and the Pottses' houses where my first playmates, all girls, lived. These houses down the street, though not every inhabitant was known by name to me, had each been as distinct to my childish awareness as the little troughs in the cement which led rain from their roof gutters out through   **line 8** the sidewalk to the street, and which punctuated my progress on roller skates or on my scooter. As the street sloped downward, there was a just-perceptible descent in the social scale as well: the porches got lower to the ground, and the front yards became exiguous. Over the years, there had been changes: wooden porch banisters and pillars had been replaced by wrought iron, in a vaguely Southern or Spanish style. Throughout Shillington, not only had houses I remembered as homes become stores but, stranger still, stores – Pep Conrad's up on Franklin and Second, Han Kieffer's here – had reverted to being homes. How had the residents divided up those open, shelved spaces? How did they live with all those ghostly aromas of merchandise?

19 As the writer starts to walk along Philadelphia Avenue, he feels himself to be

    A   a child again.
    B   something of an intruder.
    C   a long-term resident.
    D   a professional sociologist.

20 What is the significance of 'the little troughs in the cement' (line 8) to the writer?

    A   They were architecturally distinctive.
    B   They evoked early friendships.
    C   They indicated the status of each householder.
    D   They had once served as a measure of distance.

Bachelor Fads

Furniture designer Rick Gilbert's flat is a former curtain warehouse. It has the conventional features of the classic loft space, in this instance, exposed brickwork and gigantic doors, through which curtains were once hoisted from trains on the adjacent railway track. But Gilbert was adamant that he didn't want a brutally empty, open-plan space – for practical as much as aesthetic reasons.

'In my last place, living and working spaces were integrated. It was hard to switch off or start work in full view of the living area.'

Refusing to conform to the loft-dwelling convention of open-plan living, he broke up the space near the entrance with a giant snaking sheet of corrugated plastic. 'It hides the office, creates a hallway, and guides the eye to the kitchen in the middle of the flat. I wanted the kitchen to be a neutral zone, where I can either cook dinner for friends or make coffee for clients.'

To offset the synthetic look of his plastic screen and stainless steel kitchen, Gilbert laid the floors with a light wood. And while his futuristic chairs and sofas litter the flat, it's also stuffed with rather more sentimental and homely furniture, given to him by his parents or bought from markets.

21 Why does Rick Gilbert find his present accommodation more convenient than his last place?

   A It is handy for deliveries of materials.
   B It is suitable for entertaining clients.
   C It is easier to relax there.
   D It can be re-arranged easily.

22 How has Rick furnished his home?

   A according to artistic convention
   B according to his personal taste
   C in the style of a previous age
   D in line with contemporary fashion

Bruce Chatwin

To escape or to explore? The spur behind Bruce Chatwin's absurdly romantic nomadic existence has become something of a literary conundrum. Chatwin's life and art were strewn with secrets, subtle resonances and, it must be said, lies. But he was, for all that, a brilliant and unique writer. His first book, *In Patagonia*, published in 1977, is an awesome exercise in imagination. A travel book that reinvented travel writing, it has the animation of a thriller, the sparkle of romantic fiction and the irrepressible insight of truly extraordinary literature. Of course, even with this book, Chatwin cloaked fact with concoction; when sketching individuals and incidents, he would adjust, if not abandon, objective reality for the sake of a better twist to an anecdote, or a clean cut to the heart of what the book somehow seemed to suggest – that through travel it was possible to discover whole histories that had been lived out as if solely to excite and fascinate future explorers.

23 What point is made about the book *In Patagonia*?

   A   It is impossible to classify.
   B   It is a purely imaginary account.
   C   It is of little value to the traveller.
   D   It is an admirably original work.

24 What is the writer's purpose in this passage?

   A   A defence of Chatwin's failings.
   B   An examination of Chatwin's motives.
   C   A reappraisal of Chatwin's style.
   D   A questioning of Chatwin's integrity.

Swimming

The warm rain tumbled from the gutter in one of those midsummer downpours as I hastened across the lawn behind my house and took shelter in the pool. Breaststroking up and down, I nosed along, eyes just at water level. Each raindrop exploded in a momentary, bouncing fountain that turned into a bubble and burst. The best moments were when the storm intensified, drowning birdsong, and a haze rose off the water as though the pool itself were rising to meet the lowering sky.

It was at the height of this drenching in the summer of 1996 that the notion of a long swim through Britain began to form itself. I wanted to follow the rain on its meanderings about our land to rejoin the sea, to break out of the frustration of a lifetime doing lengths, of endlessly turning back on myself like a tiger pacing its cage.

Most of us live in a world where more and more places and things are signposted, labelled, and officially 'interpreted'. There is something about all this that is turning the reality of things into virtual reality. It is the reason why walking, cycling and swimming will always be subversive activities. They allow us to regain a sense of what is old and wild, by getting off the beaten track and breaking free of the official version of things. A swimming journey would give me access to that part of our world which, like darkness, misty woods or high mountains, still retains most mystery.

25 The incident in 1996 illustrates that, to the writer, rain is a symbol of

    A   repetitive cycles.
    B   enviable freedom.
    C   destroyed illusions.
    D   threatening power.

26 Why does the writer regard swimming as a 'subversive activity'?

    A   It involves no equipment or technology.
    B   It replicates an ancient skill.
    C   It allows direct contact with nature.
    D   It requires no official permission.

Part 3

You are going to read an article about online book reviews. Seven paragraphs have been removed from the extract. Choose from the paragraphs **A–H** the one which fits each gap (**27–33**). There is one extra paragraph which you do not need to use.

Mark your answers **on the separate answer sheet**.

Online Literary Criticism For All
Do-it-yourself literary criticism: more than just harmless fun?

From the outset, the idea of open access to the Internet was one of its guiding principles. In theory, anyone could publish a manifesto or broadcast a music channel on the Internet. In practice, however, a certain amount of technical know-how was required, at least in the early years.

| 27 | |

Amazon's egalitarian approach to book reviews – namely, that anyone could say what they liked about anything and award it up to five stars – looked, on the face of it, a brilliant idea. Each book had its own page on Amazon's site, and whenever a reader submitted a new review, it appeared automatically.

| 28 | |

Other online bookstores which also operated as large bricks-and-mortar bookshop chains provided similar features. But as the largest player, with over 80% of the online market, Amazon initially had the most customers, attracted by far the greatest number of reviews and, accordingly, encountered the most funny business.

| 29 | |

Single-word reviews, for instance, or personal attacks on the author, were not allowed. Nor were reviews that contained obscenities, gave

away the ending, or referred to other reviews. Ultimately, however, the reviewers were anonymous (they were not required to give their real names) and offending reviews were removed only if Amazon checkers noticed them. So there was plenty of scope for mischief.

| 30 | |

Authors were, in fact, provided with their own way to hold forth: by clicking on a link marked 'I am the Author, and I wish to comment on my book.' Most authors who used this feature posted jolly messages expressing their desire that browsers would buy, and enjoy, the book in question. A few even gave their email addresses, thus inviting readers to communicate directly. Yet authors who posted messages knew that while Amazon did vet them, it did not check that they really came from the author.

| 31 | |

Still, the fur really began to fly as a result of postings from readers, not writers. When James McElroy's *We've Got Spirit*, which documented a year in the life of a small-town cheerleading team, was published, it was well received by the mainstream press. But many of the people mentioned in it felt betrayed, and the book's page on Amazon was an obvious outlet for their anger. Dozens of highly critical reviews were submitted – only to vanish a few days later.

32

This meant that the best place to post a silly review was on a page devoted to a less well-known book. *The Story about Ping*, a classic children's work that tells the story of a duck called Ping, was the inspiration for much geek humour, because 'ping' also happened to be the name of a software utility used to measure the degree of congestion on the Internet. One lengthy review constructed an elaborate analogy between the book's plot and the architecture of the Internet, and concluded that the book provided a 'good high-level overview' of basic networking concepts.

33

The writer George Orwell once complained that 'reviewing too many books involved constantly inventing reactions towards books about which one has no spontaneous feelings whatever'. All the more reason, then, to regard the democratisation of the process as a good thing.

A Despite this episode, as far as Amazon was concerned, the fact that so many people were prepared to invest so much time reading and writing reviews was simply good for business. As readers' reviews were supposed to be a 'forum to talk about a book' rather than a chat room, a particularly close eye was kept on bestselling books, to ensure that all reviews played by the rules.

B One result was that some authors decided in future to extend their communication with their readership, by posting a taster of their next novel – or even serialising it. Though at that point, they realised they wanted to receive something more tangible than a review in return.

C However, there was at least one field, previously restricted to the few, that was genuinely opened up to the masses. By visiting the pages of Amazon.com, the first popular online bookshop, anyone was able to try their hand at literary criticism.

D For this critical free-for-all lent itself to subversion of various subtle and not-so-subtle kinds. Thousands of reviews were submitted each day – Amazon would not say exactly how many – so it was impractical to vet them all. Instead, a team of editors scoured the site, checking that reviews conformed to the company's guidelines.

E Such silliness was, however, the exception rather than the rule. The striking thing about the vast majority of reader reviews at Amazon.com was how seriously their contributors took them. And overall the reviews collectively provided a remarkably accurate indication of whether or not a particular set of goods was worth buying.

F An exception to this was made in the case of big names. A little-known writer submitted an author's comment, purporting to be from John Updike, in which he admitted to being a 'talented but ultimately over-hyped middlebrow author'. Unsurprisingly, it was deemed a fake and was removed.

G For example, there was nothing to stop writers giving their own books glowing reviews. One writer, Lev Grossman, was so mortified by the bad reviews that readers gave his first novel ('infantile trash', 'puerile pap') that he submitted several anonymous ones of his own ('hilarious', 'fabulous') to redress the balance. His ruse succeeded until he wrote an article detailing his deception. The fake reviews were promptly removed.

H This meant that Amazon got to fill its pages with free reviews, and potential buyers of a book could see what other readers thought of it, for better or worse, rather than reading just the blurb from the publisher and the views of professional critics.

Part 4

You are going to read an extract from a book on photography. For questions **34–40**, choose the answer (**A**, **B**, **C** or **D**) which you think fits best according to the text.

Mark your answers **on the separate answer sheet**.

Photography

Over the past one and a half centuries, photography has been used to record all aspects of human life and activity. During this relatively short history, the medium has expanded its capabilities in the recording of time and space, thus allowing human vision to be able to view the fleeting moment or to visualise both the vast and the minuscule. It has brought us images from remote areas of the world, distant parts of the solar system, as well as the social complexities and crises of modern life. Indeed, the photographic medium has provided one of the most important and influential means of expressing the human condition.

Nonetheless, the recording of events by means of the visual image has a much longer history. The earliest creations of pictorial recording go as far back as the Upper Palaeolithic period of about 35,000 years ago. And although we cannot be sure of the exact purposes of the early cave paintings – whether they record the 'actual' events of hunting, whether they functioned as sympathetic magic to encourage the increase of animals for hunting, whether they had a role as religious icons, or if they were made simply to enliven and brighten domestic activities – pictorial images seem to be inextricably linked to human culture as we understand it.

Throughout the history of visual representation, questions have been raised concerning the supposed accuracy (or otherwise) of the visual image, as well as its status in society. The popular notion that 'seeing is believing' had always afforded special status to the visual image. So when the technology was invented, in the form of photography, the social and cultural impact was immense.

In the mid-nineteenth century, the invention of photography appeared to offer the promise of 'automatically' providing a truthful visual record. It was seen not only as the culmination of Western visual representation but, quite simply, the camera, functioning in much the same way as the human eye, was regarded as a machine which could provide a fixed image. And this image was considered to be a very close approximation to that which we actually see. The chemical fixing of the image enabled the capture of what might be considered a natural phenomenon: the camera image. At the same time, the photographic image was held to be an achievement of sophisticated culture and produced the type of image that artists had struggled throughout the centuries to acquire the manual, visual and conceptual skills to create.

It may seem a further irony that, because of the camera's perceived realism in its ability to replicate visual perception, it was assumed that all peoples would 'naturally' be able to understand photographs. This gave rise to the question of whether photography constituted a 'universal language'. For example, in 1933 this view had been expressed in a series of radio broadcasts by photographer August Sander: 'Even the most isolated Bushman could understand a photograph of the heavens – whether it showed the sun and moon or the constellations.' However, in the face of the rapid increase in global communications which characterised the latter part of the twentieth century, we do at least need to ask to what extent the photographic image can penetrate through cultural differences in understanding. Or is photography as bound by cultural conventions as any other form of communication, such as language?

Is it possible that our familiarity with the photographic image has bred our current contempt for the intricacies and subtle methods that characterise the medium's ability to transmit its vivid impressions of 'reality'? Photography is regarded quite naturally as offering such convincing forms of pictorial evidence that this process of communication often seems to render the medium totally transparent, blurring the distinction between our perception of the environment and its photographic representations. It is the most natural thing in the world for someone to open their wallet and produce a photograph saying 'this is my grandson'.

Ever since its invention in 1839, the technology of photography and the attitudes towards the medium by its practitioners have changed radically. This may partly be attributed to photography gradually moving into what might be termed 'mythic time' – its initial role as a nineteenth-century record-keeper has now moved beyond the human scale and photographic images, once immediate and close to photographer and subject alike, have now passed out of living memory. The passage of time has transformed the photograph from a memory aid into an historical document, one which often reveals as much (if not more) about the individuals and society which produced the image as it does about its subject.

I hope to show that the camera is not merely a mute, passive chronicler of events, and that photography does not just passively reflect culture, but can provide the vision and impetus that promote social and political change and development. For example, it is difficult to imagine the cultural changes of the Italian Renaissance of the fifteenth century without recognising the central role of the development of perspective in bringing about new visual means of representation. Similarly, photography has made a major contribution to the bringing about of the media culture that characterises our own era, while at the same time it has assumed the ironic role of bringing the harsh realities of the world to the coffee-table.

34 According to the writer, how has photography contributed to our lives?

A It alters the course of significant events.
B It enables us to see humanity in a more imaginative way.
C It offers us a wide-ranging perspective.
D It influences other technological developments.

35 The writer uses the example of the Upper Palaeolithic period to underline

A the durability of pictorial representations.
B the continuity of artistic forms.
C the original function of decorative art.
D the fundamental significance of visual images.

36 In the mid-nineteenth century, the camera succeeded in

    A   acquiring scientific status.
    B   winning over a sceptical public.
    C   showing reality with a new accuracy.
    D   invalidating the work of artists.

37 What does the writer question in paragraph 5?

    A   The universal accessibility of photographic images.
    B   The effect of photography on language.
    C   The artistic value of photography in a changing world.
    D   The role of the photographer in interpreting images.

38 What point is the writer making about present-day photography in paragraph 6?

    A   We find it over-complicated.
    B   We are apt to confuse it with reality.
    C   It makes us insensitive to our surroundings.
    D   It is insubstantial compared to other art forms.

39 In what sense have some photographs moved into 'mythic time'?

    A   They have grown indistinct with age.
    B   They lack supporting documentary information.
    C   They no longer serve as an accurate record.
    D   They are obsolete in terms of their original purpose.

40 In comparing the Italian Renaissance to today's 'media culture', the writer shows photography as

    A   a social mirror.
    B   a dynamic force.
    C   an instrument of satire.
    D   an essential record.

PAPER 2   WRITING (2 hours)

Part 1

You **must** answer this question. Write your answer in **300–350** words in an appropriate style.

---

1 The extract below comes from an article which you have read in a magazine called *Society Today*. You have strong feelings about the content of the article, and decide to write a letter to the Editor in which you respond to the points made and express your own views.

> Popular culture – which includes the media, sport and the fashion industry – places great emphasis on the importance of image and appearance. This influence is producing a generation of people who are superficial, self-centred and materialistic.

Write your **letter**. Do not write any postal addresses.

Part 2

Write an answer to **one** of the questions **2−5** in this part. Write your answer in **300−350** words in an appropriate style.

---

2   The Arts Section of a national daily newspaper is doing a series of reviews on children's fiction. You decide to submit a review of ONE children's novel or collection of stories you read during childhood. In your review you should explain why your chosen work had such a strong impact on you, and comment on whether it would appeal to children today.
Write your **review**.

3   The *History Magazine* is planning to run a series of articles called 'Life in the Past'. The Editor has asked for contributions which will give an idea of what it was like to live in the past. You decide to send in an article, describing the period you would have liked to live in and giving reasons why.
Write your **article**.

4   The committee of your local sports club has decided to produce a special newsletter designed to attract new members. You have been asked to write a report of the past year's activities covering such aspects as training sessions, matches and competitions, and social events. You should mention future plans and encourage those interested to come along and find out more.
Write your **report**.

5   Based on your reading of **one** of these books, write on **one** of the following.

(a) Anne Tyler: *The Accidental Tourist*
Muriel is described as unpredictable, extreme and sometimes unlikeable. Write an essay for your tutor in which you discuss why, in view of this description of Muriel, Macon decides to go back to her at the end of *The Accidental Tourist*.
Write your **essay**.

(b) John Wyndham: *The Day of the Triffids*
A magazine is producing a series of articles entitled 'Everybody likes a story with a happy ending'. You decide to send in a review of *The Day of the Triffids*, outlining the difficulties facing Josella and Bill, and discussing whether you think the book could be described as having a happy ending or not.
Write your **review**.

(c) Graham Greene: *Our Man in Havana*
The Drama Department at your college is going to produce a stage version of *Our Man in Havana*, and has been discussing whether or not Hawthorne and the Chief should be portrayed in a serious light. The producer has asked you to write a report on whether or not these two characters are intended to be taken seriously.
Write your **report**.

Visual materials for Paper 5

1A

1B

1C

2A

2B

2C

2D

2E

2F

3A

3B

3C

3D

3E

3F

4A

TEST 1

Prompt Card 1a

In what ways are we influenced by the media?

- quality of information
- quantity of information
- advertising

TEST 2

Prompt Card 2a

How do we learn the difference between right and wrong?

- people
- education
- experience

TEST 3

Prompt Card 3a

Why do people say the world is getting smaller?

- accessing information
- travel opportunities
- international business

TEST 4

Prompt Card 4a

How do we decide what people should be paid for their jobs?

- competition
- expertise and ability
- as motivation

TEST 1

Prompt Card 1b

In what ways are people influenced during their teenage years?

- fashions
- career plans
- peer groups

TEST 2

Prompt Card 2b

In what ways have our ideas of right and wrong changed?

- science and technology
- media
- sport

TEST 3

Prompt Card 3b

How far is it true that travel broadens the mind?

- for tourists
- for workers
- for the host country

TEST 4

Prompt Card 4b

How should schools help to prepare young people for the world of work?

- areas of knowledge
- realistic expectations
- personal qualities

TEST 4

What's better – to be self employed or to be an employee?

- **the purpose of work**
- **freedom and responsibility**
- **technology**

PAPER 3   USE OF ENGLISH (1 hour 30 minutes)

Part 1

For questions **1–15**, read the text below and think of the word which best fits each space. Use only **one** word in each space. There is an example at the beginning **(0)**.

Write your answers in CAPITAL LETTERS **on the separate answer sheet**.

Example: | 0 | N | O | T | | | | | | | | | | | | | | | | | | |

RELAXATION

True relaxation is most certainly **(0)** ....*not*.... a matter of flopping down in front of the television with a welcome drink. Nor is it about drifting **(1)** .... an exhausted sleep. Useful though these responses to tension and over-tiredness **(2)** .... be, we should distinguish between them and conscious relaxation in **(3)** .... of quality and effect. **(4)** .... of the level of tiredness, real relaxation is a state of alert yet at the same **(5)** .... passive awareness, in which our bodies are **(6)** .... rest while our minds are awake.

Moreover, it is as natural **(7)** .... a healthy person to be relaxed when moving as resting. **(8)** .... relaxed in action means we bring the appropriate energy to everything we do, **(9)** .... as to have a feeling of healthy tiredness by the end of the day, **(10)** .... than one of exhaustion.

Unfortunately, as a **(11)** .... of living in today's competitive world, we are under constant strain and have difficulty in coping, **(12)** .... alone nurturing our body's abilities. **(13)** .... needs to be rediscovered is conscious relaxation. With **(14)** .... in mind we must apply ourselves to understanding stress and the nature of its causes, **(15)** .... deep-seated.

Part 2

For questions **16–25**, read the text below. Use the word given in capitals at the end of some of the lines to form a word that fits in the space in the same line. There is an example at the beginning **(0)**.

Write your answers in CAPITAL LETTERS **on the separate answer sheet**.

Example: | 0 | P | R | A | C | T | I | C | A | L | | | | | | | | | | | |

THE CONTINUING POPULARITY OF THE FOUNTAIN PEN

The fountain pen is still a very attractive and **(0)** ..practical.. object, even in   **PRACTICE**

these days of cheap, **(16)** .... ball-point and felt-tip pens. Few owners are   **DISPOSE**

(17) .... to it. Emotions range from a casual attraction to absolute passion.   **DIFFER**

However, though the reasons for such profound **(18)** .... to the pen are   **ATTACH**

many, the way people feel is universal.

What exactly is it then about this small **(19)** .... object that provokes such   **CYLINDER**

(20) .... of feeling? The most likely answer to this question is that   **INTENSE**

(21) ...., the fountain pen is far more than a mere writing instrument. It is   **BASE**

often seen as an **(22)** .... of the owner's social standing. For some, the   **ASSERT**

ornamentation is where its **(23)** .... attraction lies. It can be adorned with   **DOUBT**

gold, with diamonds or inlaid with floral or geometric designs.

A fountain pen should only be loaned out in **(24)** .... circumstances, since   **EXCEPT**

in no time at all it will be altered by the second user's hand. This is one of the

(25) .... characteristics of the instrument, which makes each one unique   **DISTINCT**

and personal to its owner.

Part 3

For questions **26–31**, think of **one** word only which can be used appropriately in all three sentences. Here is an example **(0)**.

Example:

0 Some of the tourists are hoping to get compensation for the poor state of the hotel, and I think they have a very .... case.

There's no point in trying to wade across the river, the current is far too ....

If you're asking me which of the candidates should get the job, I'm afraid I don't have any .... views either way.

0	S	T	R	O	N	G														

Write **only** the missing word in CAPITAL LETTERS **on the separate answer sheet**.

---

26 I'm sure Tom will take all these points into .... before he makes a decision.

Paul gave us an interesting .... of his trip when he returned.

Alison regretted having taken so much trouble on Basil's ....

27 Despite strong opposition, our local football team has managed to .... their position at the top of their league.

Some people .... the belief that the best parents are those that give their children the freedom to make their own choices.

The Town Council has arranged to .... a public meeting next week.

28 Buying books over the internet has changed the .... of the bookselling world completely.

James laid the playing cards .... down on the table and stared hard at his opponent.

The climbers decided to tackle the more challenging south .... of the mountain.

29 Could you give me a very .... idea of what the building work would cost?

It was an extremely .... crossing and everyone on board the little ferry felt apprehensive.

Thomas grew up in a rather .... part of Melchester and had some dubious friends.

30 Most companies will .... reasonable travelling expenses, provided that receipts are kept.

Villages are often established where two rivers ...., because this offers their inhabitants ideal conditions for trade.

With rapid developments in genetics, the sports world will soon .... new challenges, as athletes use this technology to enhance their performance.

31 The heating's off, it's no .... you're cold.

Penicillin is considered one of the .... drugs of modern medicine.

The children stared at the magician in absolute .... as he produced a song-bird from his hat.

Part 4

For questions **32–39**, complete the second sentence so that it has a similar meaning to the first sentence, using the word given. **Do not change the word given.** You must use between **three** and **eight** words, including the word given.

Here is an example **(0)**.

Example:

0 Do you .... you while you paint?

objection

0	have any objection to my watching

Write **only** the missing words **on the separate answer sheet**.

---

32 If only I hadn't believed his lies!

taken

I wish .... by his lies!

33 The committee said there was no possibility of discussing the matter any further.

discussion

The committee said that further ....
question.

34 The stranded climber would never have been rescued if his brother hadn't had an ingenious plan.

ingenuity

But .... plan, the stranded climber would never have been rescued.

35 Alison bought the big house because she wanted to open a hotel.

view

Alison bought the big house .... a hotel.

36 The writer's terse writing style contrasted sharply with his spoken language.

contrast

There .... the writer's spoken language and his terse written style.

37 It is not very likely that Angela will be given the leading role.

chance

Angela has .... the leading role.

38 When I started work I was so inexperienced that I couldn't send a fax.

clue

I didn't .... send a fax when I started work.

39 It took several months for George to recover completely from his accident.

make

Only after several months .... his accident.

Part 5

For questions **40–44**, read the following texts about work. For questions **40–43**, answer with a word or short phrase. You do not need to write complete sentences. For question **44**, write a summary according to the instructions given.

Write your answers to questions **40–44 on the separate answer sheet**.

Be it a data entry, a deleted file or a jammed photocopier, every office is susceptible to the occasional human hiccup. At best, mistakes are time- **line 2** consuming and costly; at worst they are fatal. Several recent disasters have been attributed to employee oversights, a fact that has forced companies to consider how best to handle slips and lapses. Traditionally, employers have taken a punitive line, but a recent study has shown that it might be in the company's interest to embrace employees who blunder. 'Rewarding staff for managing errors rather than punishing them leads to a better company culture,' says one researcher whose work has revealed a relationship between error tolerance and commercial success.

A psychologist who looks at human errors in work settings where safety is critical adds: 'If you have a work system that is error intolerant, the efficiency of an organisation is going to be affected. If someone is in a situation where a flick of a button means the entire contents of the computer are wiped, then that person is likely to lead a fairly stressful life. If you can set up a system designed to be error tolerant, you're likely to see less of the normal human psyche protection **line 16** strategies. People understandably look elsewhere for explanations when things go wrong, but if systems are set up correctly and people know their actions will be recoverable, they can be more innovative and express themselves in their work without fear of getting the blame for every little thing that goes wrong.'

40 Which two other phrases from paragraph 1 express the same idea as 'occasional human hiccup' (line 2)?

....

41 In your own words say what the writer means when she uses the phrase 'human psyche protection strategies' (lines 16–17).

....

Not so long ago, stressed-out executives at a failing company were packed off on a training course. Nothing so very unusual about that, but they were in for a surprise. There was no time management seminar, no flashy flip-charts. Instead they were faced with cardboard, paint and glue. The day-long session required each delegate to create a mask to represent the face they presented at work. Mask-making, it is claimed, is a very effective corporate tool. It helps people access their intuitive, imaginative skills.

Creativity has become a highly-prized commodity, even in less-than-fizzy professions   **line 7** such as accountancy. Bosses have begun to see that if you sit in a boring meeting in a boring conference room, you will inevitably emerge with boring ideas. As companies become desperate to harness creativity and lateral thinking, they are being forced to look at new ways of fostering those talents. A London comedy club has launched a corporate programme to inspire executives by teaching them to do comic routines, because forward-looking companies realise a good atmosphere at work and good relations with colleagues are crucial to motivating staff. Teaching them how to laugh with each other is a good start. There are other courses that focus on humour in the belief that comedy can help employees confront their inner fears. Says the organiser, 'We get people to write a story about a situation that's bothering them, then we clown it. It's not about being funny, it's about developing self-expression.'

42 Explain in your own words why the training course mentioned in paragraph 1 did not match the participants' expectations.

....

43 What does the writer's use of the phrase 'less-than-fizzy' (line 7) reveal about her attitude to accountancy?

....

44 In a paragraph of between **50** and **70** words, summarise **in your own words as far as possible** the methods described in the texts which employers use to get the best out of their staff. **Write your summary on the separate answer sheet**.

PAPER 4   LISTENING (40 minutes approximately)

Part 1

You will hear four different extracts. For questions **1–8**, choose the answer (**A**, **B** or **C**) which fits best according to what you hear. There are two questions for each extract.

Extract 1

You hear a radio interview with a woman who runs a fish farm in Wales.

1 The farmer says she breeds her own fish because

  A it is important for her to be independent of suppliers.
  B her clients require records of the fishes' history.
  C that is the most satisfying part of the process for her.

                                                            1

2 Why does she say she stays in fish farming?

  A Doing her best for her customers is satisfying.
  B Her skills are not transferable to other businesses.
  C She has built up an extremely profitable business.

                                                            2

Extract 2

You hear a novelist being interviewed about her early career.

3 How does she feel about the scarcity of women writers in literary reviews and journals?

  A depressed
  B unconcerned
  C discouraged

                                                            3

4 Why does the speaker think the novel is a good vehicle for woman writers?

  A The best novel writers have tended to be women.
  B Her own attempts at drama did not meet with success.
  C There is a body of recognised work by female writers.

                                                            4

Extract 3

You hear two people talking about a character from a book.

5 The man describes the character of Inspector Rebus by

   A   comparing his anxieties to those of ordinary people.
   B   pointing out his interest in global issues.
   C   emphasising his problem-solving abilities.

6 According to the man, a police detective may be motivated by

   A   a desire to achieve justice.
   B   a wish to make sense of life.
   C   a need to explore his inner self.

Extract 4

You hear a music journalist talking about changes in popular youth culture in Britain.

7 According to the journalist the main role of pop music in the 1960s was

   A   to help young people be less self-conscious.
   B   to inspire teenage relationships.
   C   to facilitate the growing-up process.

8 The change in youth culture in the 1960s meant that

   A   parents acted as role models for their teenage children.
   B   young people gained responsibility for their lives earlier.
   C   the older generation struggled to keep their values.

Part 2

You will hear a lecture on the cork forests of southern Spain and Portugal. For questions **9–17**, complete the sentences with a word or short phrase.

Cork trees need earth which is | **9** | to grow well.

One tree can be harvested up to a | **10** | times.

The main product made from poor quality cork is | **11** |

Healthy growth is primarily maintained by appropriate | **12** | of the cork tree.

Bio-diversity in cork-growing areas is maintained by planting | **13** | between the trees.

The speaker believes that the contaminant TCA is spread from the | **14** | of other trees.

The Cork Growers' Association has agreed to use contaminated cork for | **15** |

Decline in the cork forests will make a | **16** | of the area.

The habitat of rare animals such as the | **17** | will be lost if the forests decline.

Part 3

You will hear part of a radio programme about a group of people on an expedition to the South Pole. For questions **18–22**, choose the answer (**A**, **B**, **C** or **D**) which fits best according to what you hear.

---

18 The team members do not talk to each other while they walk because they

    A wear protective head-gear.
    B walk one behind the other.
    C use a lot of energy pulling heavily laden sledges.
    D find it difficult to keep momentum going.

> **18**

19 This expedition is different from the one to the North Pole because it is

    A all-female.
    B less rigorous.
    C not a relay.
    D shorter.

> **19**

20 Caroline's confidence was severely dented when

    A there were tremors underneath them.
    B one of the team injured her shoulder.
    C they came across a crevasse for the first time.
    D one of the sledges crashed into a crevasse.

> **20**

21 What does Caroline say about the team's sleeping patterns?

    A It is not easy to sleep because it's so cold.
    B They sleep soundly.
    C They are usually awake when the alarm rings.
    D They do not get enough sleep.

> **21**

22 It is easy for Caroline to accept the other team's success because

    A it was on a fund-raising expedition.
    B it is more experienced.
    C its make-up is different.
    D its members are their friends.

> **22**

Part 4

You will hear part of a radio programme in which two people, Louise and Stephen, discuss a film they have recently seen. For questions **23–28**, decide whether the opinions are expressed by only one of the speakers, or whether the speakers agree.

Write   **L**   for Louise
       S   for Stephen
or   **B**   for Both, where they agree.

---

23   The film is a successful satire on the 'American Dream'.   **23**

24   Many of the images seem commonplace.   **24**

25   Although the main topics are by no means new, they've been given a different slant.   **25**

26   There were some truly exceptional passages in the film.   **26**

27   The ending of the film is inconclusive.   **27**

28   In terms of pace, the film is well judged.   **28**

PAPER 5   SPEAKING (19 minutes)

There are two examiners. One (the Interlocutor) conducts the test, providing you with the necessary materials and explaining what you have to do. The other examiner (the Assessor) will be introduced to you, but then takes no further part in the interaction.

Part 1 (3 minutes)

The Interlocutor first asks you and your partner a few questions which focus on information about yourselves and personal opinions.

Part 2 (4 minutes)

In this part of the test you and your partner are asked to talk together. The Interlocutor places a set of pictures on the table in front of you. This stimulus provides the basis for a discussion. The Interlocutor first asks an introductory question which focuses on one or two of the pictures. After about a minute, the Interlocutor gives you both a decision-making task based on the same set of pictures.

The pictures for Part 2 are on pages C6–C7 of the colour section.

Part 3 (12 minutes)

You are each given the opportunity to talk for two minutes, to comment after your partner has spoken and to take part in a more general discussion.

The Interlocutor gives you a card with a question written on it and asks you to talk about it for two minutes. After you have spoken, your partner is first asked to comment and then the Interlocutor asks you both another question related to the topic on the card. This procedure is repeated, so that your partner receives a card and speaks for two minutes, you are given an opportunity to comment and a follow-up question is asked.

Finally, the Interlocutor asks some further questions, which leads to a discussion on a general theme related to the subjects already covered in Part 3.

The cards for Part 3 are on pages C10–C11 of the colour section.

Test 4

PAPER 1   READING (1 hour 30 minutes)

Part 1

For questions **1–18**, read the three texts below and decide which answer (**A**, **B**, **C** or **D**) best fits each gap.

Mark your answers **on the separate answer sheet**.

Clutter

Sometimes it seems that no matter how many possessions you have, you never feel secure. While it is reasonable to have a basic nesting instinct and create a home which **(1)** .... your needs, there is a point where the motivation for acquiring things gets out of control. Modern advertising is **(2)** .... deliberately designed to play on our insecurities. 'If you don't have one of these you will be a **(3)** .... human being' is one of the consistent **(4)** .... messages we receive. To discover just how much you are influenced, I challenge you to try not to read any advertising billboards next time you go down the street. These multi-million dollar messages **(5)** .... condition us in very persuasive ways without our ever realising it. We are bombarded by them – television, radio, newspapers, magazines, posters, tee shirts, the internet, you **(6)** .... it – all encouraging us to buy, buy, buy.

1 A	quenches	**B**	stays	**C**	meets	**D**	feeds
2 A	nonetheless	**B**	moreover	**C**	thereby	**D**	whatever
3 A	minor	**B**	lesser	**C**	deeper	**D**	lower
4 A	subdued	**B**	submerged	**C**	underlying	**D**	underhand
5 A	relentlessly	**B**	fiercely	**C**	thoroughly	**D**	extremely
6 A	label	**B**	tell	**C**	say	**D**	name

Caves

Research establishments and university departments around the world have **(7)** .... years of research time in all aspects of caves, mainly their origins, their hydrology and their biology. Caves constitute a small but rather mysterious **(8)** .... of the natural environment – as such they **(9)** .... our curiosity and challenge our desire for knowledge, and consequently have had a considerable

83

amount of research effort **(10)** .... to them. Furthermore, because of their presence as natural phenomena, they have had a long history of study, which has been intensified in those parts of the world where caves have had a direct effect on our way of life. However, the physical **(11)** .... required to visit many caves means that cave research has been less in the hands of the learned professors than in most other scientific fields. Indeed there is a considerable, perhaps unique, **(12)** .... between the professional, scientific study of caves and the amateur studies carried out by those who mainly visit caves for sport.

7 A	conducted	**B**	done	**C**	invested	**D**	made
8 A	constituent	**B**	compartment	**C**	complement	**D**	component
9 A	arouse	**B**	incite	**C**	tempt	**D**	instigate
10 A	donated	**B**	bestowed	**C**	devoted	**D**	lavished
11 A	agility	**B**	capacity	**C**	properties	**D**	demands
12 A	underlay	**B**	overlap	**C**	stratification	**D**	dependence

Weather Watch

Countless observant people without any instruments other than their own senses originally **(13)** .... the foundations of meteorology, which has progressed since the 17th century into the highly technical science of today. Satellites and electronic instruments **(14)** .... endless weather information to us with the minimum of delay, computers solve in minutes abstruse mathematical sums at a speed beyond the capability of the human brain. Meteorological theory is peppered with long words which have little **(15)** .... to the non-professional. It sometimes seems there is no room left for simple weather wisdom, but nothing could be further from the **(16)** .... . Human experience is still the vital ingredient which **(17)** .... computed data into weather forecasts. Human observations can still provide unusual evidence which is of great help to professionals who are trying to **(18)** .... the mysteries of the atmosphere.

13 A	spread	**B**	made	**C**	put	**D**	laid
14 A	relay	**B**	diffuse	**C**	share	**D**	deal
15 A	purpose	**B**	validity	**C**	meaning	**D**	message
16 A	trust	**B**	honesty	**C**	truth	**D**	wisdom
17 A	transports	**B**	translates	**C**	transcends	**D**	transposes
18 A	untie	**B**	undo	**C**	unwrap	**D**	unravel

Part 2

You are going to read four extracts which are all concerned in some way with fine art. For questions **19–26**, choose the answer (**A**, **B**, **C** or **D**) which you think fits best according to the text.

Mark your answers **on the separate answer sheet**.

Art

In modern times – more and more over the course of the last two hundred years – we have come to speak as though every artist had to rebel against the art of his contemporaries. Art is praised in terms of being unique, revolutionary, shocking even. We feel good about admiring the artist whose work no one appreciated a hundred years ago. But when we get to the art of our own day, we get cold feet and say that an artist has gone too far, that what he does can no longer be called art. Or, rather, the media say it for us. And, on the whole, we agree because we expect to be puzzled by art's insistent newness – so much so that we do not notice the old themes, methods and also virtues that the art of our own time is full of.

We require artists to be separate from the rest of us, figures with special talents and drive, so vigorous that conventions cannot contain them. Previous ages went to artists with commissions: people needed art for specific purposes, and it was part of their ordinary life. Today we leave artists to their own devices and get rather cross with them if they want to come down out of the clouds.

19 According to the writer, how do people react to modern art these days?

   A in an unrestrained way
   B in an illogical way
   C in an unconventional way
   D in an unpredictable way

20 In the second paragraph, the writer makes the point that artists are no longer regarded as people with

   A a message to impart.
   B an unusual lifestyle.
   C a role in society.
   D a functional skill.

Picture This

I am going to describe a situation, and then ask a crucial question about it. I hope it doesn't strike you as unduly gnomic. But if it does, that's modern art for you.

Here's the situation. An artist chooses a piece of text in an art book. The text considers the diversity of pictures. 'What are they all about?' it asks dumbly, before deciding, even more dumbly: 'There is no end, in fact, to the number of different kinds of pictures.' Okay, this is kiddy-language, and so far all it has betrayed is kiddy-thinking. But stick with me, all you adults out there. The situation is about to complicate itself.

Having settled on his text, the man then asks someone else to make a canvas for him, to stretch it and prime it, and then to take it along to a sign painter. He asks the sign painter to write the chosen text on the canvas. And he gives the sign painter specific instructions not to attempt anything flashy or charming with the lettering. The sign painter does all this. On a white canvas, in simple black letters, he writes the chosen text. So my crucial question is this: is the finished product a painting?

21 What is the writer's purpose in paragraph 2?

   A   to patronise the reader
   B   to deny a contradiction
   C   to trivialise a concept
   D   to insult artists in general

22 What is called into question in the final paragraph?

   A   the validity of the work of art
   B   the reputation of the artist
   C   the quality of the materials
   D   the skill of the sign painter

Underground Encounters

At the Mercury Gallery, London until 26th June

It is an unspoken rule of commercial success as a painter that once you have developed a profitable line in one genre, you stick to it. Collectors expect an artist to diligently mine the same seam, and attempts to strike out in a new direction are usually met at best with indignation and the feeling that the artist has let the public down.

Why this should be I'm not entirely sure. Gallery owners obviously prefer safe bets, and perhaps the art-buying public is insecure and needs the comfort of continuity. A few artists break the mould and get away with it. Picasso and Hockney are two prime examples. Eric Rimmington is another artist who is now gamely running contrary to form, and it remains to be seen if he can pull it off. His new show takes the daring step of swapping the pristine still lifes which have made his name for paintings of the world of the London Underground.

Railways hold a peculiar charm for Rimmington. From drawings made in the 1980s of the railway land of London's Kings Cross Station, it was a logical step to go beneath the ground and look at what was happening below. The sketches have provided the material for Underground Encounters, an exhibition of 40 paintings and drawings which convey the curious magic of this sunken world designed for a population in transit.

23 What point is exemplified in the text by the reference to Picasso and Hockney?

A   Art buyers tend to prefer certain individual artists or genres.
B   Artists are rarely appreciated for their commercial insight.
C   Artistic styles can be successfully changed or modified.
D   Certain artistic genres are more profitable than others.

24 In the writer's opinion, Rimmington's current choice of subject matter

A   represents a natural artistic progression.
B   is a reflection of his unconventional personality.
C   is likely to bring him even greater success as an artist.
D   represents an attempt to reach a wider artistic audience.

Extract from a novel

I have escaped to this island with a few books. I do not know why I use the word 'escape'. The villagers say jokingly that only a sick man would choose such a remote place to rebuild. Well then, I have come here to heal myself, if you like to put it that way.

Apart from the wrinkled old peasant who comes from the village on her mule each day to clean the house, I am quite alone. I am neither happy nor unhappy; I lie suspended like a hair or a feather in the cloudy mixtures of memory. I spoke of the uselessness of art but added nothing truthful about its consolations. The solace of such work as I do with brain and heart lies in this – that only *there*, in the silences of the painter or the writer can reality be   **line 10** reordered, reworked and made to show its significant side. Our common actions in reality are simply the sackcloth covering which hides the cloth-of-gold – the meaning of the pattern. For us artists there waits the joyous compromise through art with all that wounded or defeated us in daily life; in this way, not to evade destiny, as the ordinary people try to do, but to fulfil it in its true potential – the imagination. Otherwise why should we hurt one another?

25 The words 'that only *there*' in line 10 refer to the artist's

    A mind.
    B past.
    C real life.
    D physical location.

26 Which of the following best summarises what the writer says about art?

    A It offers more to the individual than is immediately apparent.
    B It provides an escape from the difficulties of everyday life.
    C It provides answers to complex social problems.
    D It clarifies the way we perceive some experiences.

Part 3

You are going to read an extract from an article about refuse collection. Seven paragraphs have been removed from the extract. Choose from the paragraphs **A–H** the one which fits each gap (**27–33**). There is one extra paragraph which you do not need to use.

Mark your answers **on the separate answer sheet**.

Garbage in, garbage out

Charging families for each bag of rubbish they produce seems environmentally sound and economically sensible. It may not be.

Some rituals of modern domestic living vary little throughout the developed world. One such is the municipal refuse collection: at regular intervals, rubbish bags or the contents of rubbish bins disappear into the bowels of a special lorry and are carried away to the local tip.

27	

Yet the cost of rubbish disposal is not zero at all. The more rubbish people throw away, the more rubbish collectors and trucks are needed, and the more the local authorities have to pay in landfill and tipping fees. This looks like the most basic of economic problems: if rubbish disposal is free, people will produce too much rubbish.

28	

But as Don Fullerton and Thomas Kinnaman, two American economists, have found, what appears to be the logical approach to an everyday problem has surprisingly intricate and sometimes disappointing results.

29	

In a paper published last year Messrs Fullerton and Kinnaman concentrated on the effects of one such scheme, introduced in July 1992 in Charlottesville, Virginia, a town of about 40,000 people. Residents were charged 80 cents for each tagged bag of rubbish. This may sound like sensible use of market forces. In fact, the authors conclude, the scheme's benefits did not cover the cost of printing materials, the commissions to sellers and the wages of the people running the scheme.

30	

As we all know, such compacting is done better by machines at landfill sites than by individuals, however enthusiastically. The weight of rubbish collected (a better indicator of disposal costs than volume) fell by a modest 14% in Charlottesville. In 25 other Virginian cities where no pricing scheme was in place, and which were used as a rough-and-ready control group, it fell by 3.5% in any case.

31	

The one bright spot in the whole experience seems to have been a 15% increase in the weight of materials recycled, suggesting that people chose to recycle (which is free) rather than pay to have their refuse carted away. But the fee may have little to do with the growth in recycling, as many citizens were already participating in Charlottesville's voluntary scheme.

32

This figure is lower than in other studies covering fewer towns, but is it so surprising? To reduce their output of rubbish by a lot, people would have to buy less of just about everything. A tax of a few cents on the week's garbage seems unlikely to make much difference.

33

Should we conclude that the idea of charging households for the rubbish they produce is daft? Not at all: free disposal after all is surely too cheap. But the effects of seemingly simple policies are often complex. Intricate economic models are often needed to sort them out. And sometimes, the results of this rummaging do not smell sweet.

A Less pleasing still, some people resorted to illegal dumping rather than pay to have their rubbish removed. This is hard to measure directly but the authors guess that illegal dumping may account for 30–40% of the reduction in collected rubbish.

B It would be foolish to generalise from this one situation. Economic incentives sometimes produce unforeseen responses. To discourage this method of waste disposal, local authorities might have to spend more on catching litterers, or raise fines.

C If that's the case, it seems worth considering whether other factors, such as income and education, matter every bit as much as price. In richer towns, for example, people throw out more rubbish than in poorer ones and they have less time for recycling.

D In a more recent study, Messrs Fullerton and Kinnaman explore the economics of rubbish in more detail. One conclusion from this broader study is that pricing does reduce the weight of rubbish – but not by much. On average, a 10% increase in sticker prices cuts quantity only by 0.3%.

E To economists, this ceremony is peculiar, because in most places it is free. Yes, households pay for the service out of local taxes but the family that fills four bins with rubbish each week pays no more than the elderly couple that fills one.

F The obvious solution is to make households pay the marginal cost of disposing of their waste. That will give them an incentive to throw out less and recycle more (assuming that local governments provide collection points for suitable materials).

G True, the number of bags or cans did fall sharply, by 37%. But this was largely thanks to the 'Seattle stomp', a frantic dance first noticed when that distant city introduced rubbish pricing. Rather than buy more tags, people simply crammed more garbage – about 40% more – into each container by jumping on it if necessary.

H Research focused on several American towns and cities which, in the past few years, have started charging households for generating rubbish. The commonest system is to sell stickers or tags which householders attach to rubbish bags or cans. Only bags with these labels are picked up in the weekly collection.

Part 4

You are going to read an article about music. For questions **34–40**, choose the answer (**A, B, C** or **D**) which you think fits best according to the text.

Mark your answers **on the separate answer sheet**.

MUSIC AND THEATRE

Up until quite recently, I would have said that opera is first and foremost theatre. Not any more. After a brief spell working at a national opera house, I learned that opera is, in fact, only secondly theatre. The music comes first. That's as it should be, of course. But I come from a different world, the world of the theatre, where the word and the actor speaking it have primacy, where there is nobody out front directing the action once the event is under way, and where performer and audience (mostly) speak the same language.

At any musical performance, whether in concert hall or opera house, there will generally be a substantial minority of people who, like me, have little technical or academic understanding of music. Some of them will be aware of, possibly even embarrassed by, how much they don't know. Most will be awestruck by the skill of the performers. A dazzling coloratura or an impeccable string section are easy to admire. Even a moderately good musician is showing us the results of years of punishingly hard work. Being in the audience for top-class music is not unlike watching an athletics match – we know athletes are doing something broadly similar to what we do when running for a bus, but we also recognise by how much it exceeds our best efforts.

Theatre audiences by contrast, come with a different set of expectations. In the main they do not understand the nature of an actor's skill and are not particularly awed by an activity which, a lot of the time, appears to be very close to what they could do themselves. They are not usually impressed when an actor completes a long and difficult speech (although 'how do you learn all those lines?' is the question every actor gets asked). None of this means that theatre audiences are more generous or less demanding than their counterparts in the concert hall; indeed quite a lot of them are the same people. What perhaps it does mean is that audiences and performer meet on more equal terms in the theatre than elsewhere, no matter how challenging the material or spectacular the event. The question is, does music need to learn anything from the theatre about this relationship? I would say yes, partly because I have seen how a different approach can transform the concert-goer's experience.

Music in live performance is inherently theatrical, full of passion, humour, melancholy, intimacy, grandeur; vulnerable to the possibility that something will go unexpectedly wrong, reaching into the imagination of the listener not just as an individual but as part of a collective. The conventions which still largely dominate music presentation, including strict dress codes and an exaggerated deference to the status of conductors and soloists, emphasise the difference between players and listeners in a way which often feels uncomfortably hierarchical. On the other hand, the tendency of contemporary music audiences to interrupt the momentum of performance by applauding between movements or after a particular piece of virtuosity, while it is often a spontaneous expression of appreciation, can also be insensitive to the dramatic integrity of the whole work.

Is there anything to be done? Of course a huge amount is being done. Pioneering work is going on all over the country to encourage new audiences into concert halls and opera houses, and to break down the barriers that make people feel that 'serious' music is not for them. I remember a remarkable event, the staging of Jonathan Dove's community opera *In Search of Angels*, which followed the action from location to location within a cathedral and then out into the town. It was a musical experience of the highest order, in which the skills, and the generosity, of the professional musicians were absolutely central and it was also life-changing for many of the audience, who were not just there to see and hear but also to contribute directly.

Perhaps what I yearn for in music is a bit more of the risk and radicalism that theatre at its best can display. Sometimes it can come from the use of unfamiliar or challenging locations, where normal expectations are disrupted. This can have startling effects on performer and audience alike. Comforts may have to be foregone; perhaps the acoustic isn't great, maybe it's a bit cold, but theatre audiences have learned to be intrepid as they follow artists into the most unpromising spaces. I accept that most plays get put on in a pretty uncontroversial way, not greatly different from what happens in a concert hall. However I remain convinced that something can and should happen to change the conventions of music-going. The only authority I can claim is that of the enthusiast: I love, and live by, the theatre and I spend as much time (and money) as I can going to hear music. I want them both to thrive, and for more and more people to get the pleasure I get from being the audience.

34 What does the writer imply in the first paragraph?

    A She finds opera difficult to appreciate.
    B She recognises some shortcomings of the theatre.
    C She has re-evaluated her view of opera.
    D She is reluctant to change her view of the theatre.

35 The writer says that a significant number of people who attend musical performances may

    A lack her specialist knowledge.
    B have a sense of inadequacy.
    C be unimpressed by the musicians' talent.
    D make no attempts to engage with the music.

36 What point is exemplified by the reference to athletes in the second paragraph?

    A Musicians have to train for longer than athletes.
    B Athletes find performing in public demanding.
    C Audiences recognise the particular talent of the musicians.
    D It is harder to become an athlete than a musician.

37 What does the writer say about theatre audiences?

    A Their assumptions are different from concert audiences.
    B They regard the actor's technique as crucial.
    C Their appraisal of performances is realistic.
    D They are less critical than concert audiences.

38 What is the writer's attitude towards the conventions surrounding musical performance?

    A It is unreasonable to expect instant changes.
    B They enable the audience to show respect for the performers.
    C It is important to retain some traditions.
    D They can result in a feeling of divisiveness.

39 What was it about the staging of *In Search of Angels* that impressed the writer?

    A the size of the auditorium
    B the absence of commercial motivation
    C the composition of the audience
    D the opportunity for audience participation

40 In the final paragraph, the writer expresses a desire to see more

    A cooperation between musicians and actors.
    B suitable facilities at venues.
    C challenging music in theatrical performances.
    D innovation in musical performances.

PAPER 2 WRITING (2 hours)

Part 1

You **must** answer this question. Write your answer in **300–350** words in an appropriate style.

---

1 You read the extract below taken from an interview in a media magazine. The Editor has invited readers to contribute articles entitled 'Books – An Endangered Species?'. Write an article responding to the issues raised and expressing your own views.

> Some people believe that books are an endangered species, fighting for survival in competition with TV, film, the Internet and CD Roms. But I believe books provide unique intellectual pleasures. The mind is free to create its own images, rather than passively receiving them from a TV or computer screen. It's just as easy to open a book as it is to switch on the TV or computer, and often more convenient.

Write your **article**.

Part 2

Write an answer to **one** of the questions **2–5** in this part. Write your answer in **300–350** words in an appropriate style.

---

2   A television company is looking for people who would be willing to spend six months on a desert island with 20 others. The participants will have to survive without electricity, telephone and other modern devices, and their experiences will be filmed for a future programme. Write a letter saying why you would like to take part and what you would hope to learn from the experience. Write your **letter**. Do not write any postal addresses.

3   You see a poster on your college notice board about celebrating the end of the academic year. The Student Social Committee has made some suggestions – a dinner, a disco, a concert – and has asked for other ideas. You decide to send in a proposal, commenting on these possibilities, and stating which idea you think would be the best and why. Write your **proposal**.

4   A film magazine is producing a series of reviews called 'The Funniest Films Ever Made'. You decide to send in a review. In your review, describe briefly what happens in the film, say what makes the film particularly successful, and why you think it should be considered the funniest film ever made. Write your **review**.

5   Based on your reading of **one** of these books, write on **one** of the following.

   (a) Anne Tyler: *The Accidental Tourist*
   A recent series of articles in a literary magazine has been dealing with the theme of animals in literature. In one of the articles it was said 'A dog cannot possibly have a significant role in a novel for adults'. You write a letter in which you discuss this comment with reference to the dog, Edward, and the role he plays in *The Accidental Tourist*.
   Write your **letter**. Do not write any postal addresses.

   (b) John Wyndham: *The Day of the Triffids*
   Your tutor has asked you to write an essay comparing Tynsham with Shirning, making reference to the people there and the way they organise their lives. Say how these people and places affected Bill Masen.
   Write your **essay**.

   (c) Graham Greene: *Our Man in Havana*
   Your class has been studying *Our Man in Havana*, and your tutor has asked you to write an essay on the theme 'Loyalty, rather than patriotism, is the message of this novel'. Consider the statement with reference to the characters and actions of Hawthorne and Wormold.
   Write your **essay**.

PAPER 3   USE OF ENGLISH (1 hour 30 minutes)

Part 1

For questions **1–15**, read the text below and think of the word which best fits each space. Use only **one** word in each space. There is an example at the beginning **(0)**.

Write your answers in CAPITAL LETTERS **on the separate answer sheet**.

Example: `0` `W` `H` `I` `C` `H`

ANIMAL IMPRINTING

Imprinting is a learning mechanism **(0)** *which* occurs early in the life of certain animals. **(1)** ....
is through this process that they develop a positive attachment **(2)** .... members of their own
species. No **(3)** .... do young birds hatch than they must learn to recognise their mother in
(4) .... to be able to follow and keep close to her for their own safety. **(5)** .... this process go
wrong, newly-hatched chicks **(6)** .... the risk of becoming lost, and may **(7)** .... to harm.
(8) .... that they possess a high level of mobility, it would be difficult for the mother to keep the
chicks together **(9)** .... the assistance of imprinting. The process can take literally **(10)** ....
matter of minutes. The first large moving object the chicks see **(11)** .... automatically become
'mother'. In normal circumstances, of course, **(12)** .... really is their mother, but under
experimental conditions it can be almost **(13)** .... For instance, **(14)** .... the moving object
happens to be an orange balloon on a piece of string, then the balloon becomes 'mother'. So
powerful is this imprinting process that even after a few days, and **(15)** .... the presence of their
real mother, the chicks will choose the balloon.

Part 2

For questions **16–25**, read the text below. Use the word given in capitals at the end of some of the lines to form a word that fits in the space in the same line. There is an example at the beginning **(0)**.

Write your answers in CAPITAL LETTERS **on the separate answer sheet**.

Example: | 0 | P | S | Y | C | H | O | L | O | G | I | S | T | S | | | | | |

EVERY TIME WE SAY GOODBYE

According to research by **(0)** .psychologists. one can learn a great deal about   **PSYCHOLOGY**

the state of people's relationships by watching how they say goodbye at

airports. However, it seems that it is not **(16)** .... those in the strongest   **NECESSARY**

relationships who make the greatest display of **(17)** .... at parting. Such   **RELUCTANT**

behaviour is more **(18)** .... of couples who have been together for a relatively   **CHARACTER**

short period of time. There is less **(19)** .... of people in long-term   **LIKELY**

relationships showing strong feelings of dependency. This may seem

surprising but it is **(20)** .... because the people have been successful in   **PRESUME**

establishing stability in their relationship and are able to see the separation as

brief and of no great **(21)** ....   **SIGNIFY**

The expression of emotion at these moments may often reflect **(22)** .... and   **SECURE**

also the feeling that the person leaving is not fully **(23)** .... of just how   **APPRECIATE**

important the relationship is to the person being left. The person leaving may

also seem **(24)** .... of how unsettling a separation can be for the person left   **AWARE**

behind, who may then experience a very real sense of **(25)** ....   **LONELY**

Part 3

For questions **26–31**, think of **one** word only which can be used appropriately in all three sentences. Here is an example **(0)**.

Example:

0 Some of the tourists are hoping to get compensation for the poor state of the hotel, and I think they have a very .... case.

There's no point in trying to wade across the river, the current is far too ....

If you're asking me which of the candidates should get the job, I'm afraid I don't have any .... views either way.

0	S	T	R	O	N	G													

Write **only** the missing word in CAPITAL LETTERS **on the separate answer sheet**.

---

26 Despite the traffic problems, Joe managed to .... up for his interview on time.

I think we should .... back before it gets dark or we'll get lost.

I was sure the holiday would .... out fine in the end.

27 The government has to take .... to hold down taxation if it wants to be re-elected.

One of the guides showed the tourists the flight of .... that led down to the castle dungeon.

Our theatre group had to learn a set of very intricate .... before we could perform the local folk dance.

28 During the weekend, thieves stole a priceless .... from the gallery.

There's sound, but I can't get any .... on this TV set.

The newscaster gave an accurate .... of the tense situation caused by the transport strike.

29   The murderer's sudden .... of guilt surprised the police.

It is expected that the museum will make a financial loss this year unless prices for .... are increased.

The government's reluctant .... that the unemployment figures had risen was a shock to everyone.

30   The writing is so .... that I can hardly read it.

I'd been standing in the queue for over half an hour when I suddenly began to feel ....

There's still a .... chance that she'll get here on time if the traffic isn't too heavy.

31   The company was in difficulties and needed an injection of .... to solve its problems.

Tonight everyone in the country is converging on the .... for the New Year celebrations.

Like all politicians, he was keen to make as much .... as possible from the rumours surrounding his opponent's business dealings.

Part 4

For questions **32–39**, complete the second sentence so that it has a similar meaning to the first sentence, using the word given. **Do not change the word given.** You must use between **three** and **eight** words, including the word given.

Here is an example **(0)**.

Example:

0 Do you mind if I watch you while you paint?

objection

Do you .... you while you paint?

0	have any objection to my watching

Write **only** the missing words **on the separate answer sheet**.

---

32 Many people believe that all cats have tails, but they're wrong.

popular

Contrary .... cats have tails.

33 Alan was not a confident person, and that was why he was so shy.

due

Alan's .... of confidence.

34 'I can't believe it – I've just come into £10,000!' James shouted.

luck

James couldn't .... came into £10,000.

35 They weren't getting anywhere until John had a bright idea.

came

They were getting .... a bright idea.

36 Peter is not very aware of other people's feelings.

lacks

Peter .... comes to other people's feelings.

37 If you don't know what you're doing, you shouldn't dismantle the clock.

apart

Don't .... you know what you're doing.

38 Will Tom be able to type as well now that he's broken his thumb?

affect

Will Tom's .... to type?

39 Jane will always regret not accepting the opportunity to go to drama school.

turned

Jane will always wish that .... the opportunity to go to drama school.

Part 5

For questions **40–44**, read the following texts about live and recorded music. For questions **40–43**, answer with a word or short phrase. You do not need to write complete sentences. For question **44**, write a summary according to the instructions given.

Write your answers to questions **40–44 on the separate answer sheet**.

Music's significance for the listener at home has been greatly increased by modern methods of recording. Nevertheless, critics of recorded music are right to point out that repeated hearings of a particular performance may cause the listener to think that the interpretation to which he has become accustomed is the only one possible. Moreover, modern recording techniques, which often, though not invariably, involve repeated 'takes' of short sections of a work in order to eliminate minor flaws, may in so doing eliminate spontaneity. Great music requires an emotional commitment from performers which cannot be combined with an obsessional insistence on perfection. **line 8**

One famous pianist retired from the concert platform at the age of twenty-eight. He deplored the applause at concerts and became increasingly affected by stage fright. In any case, he thought that the concert hall would soon disappear because of progress in the technology of recording. He claimed that the listener at home, by adjusting controls to his or her personal taste, could come closer to an ideal performance and reach a depth of musical experience unattainable at a live concert.

This pianist's dislike of performing in public was rooted in his own peculiar temperament. He was predominantly solitary, preferring telephone conversations to face-to-face encounters. However, his ideas should not be dismissed lightly just because of his personal idiosyncrasies. Music can and does affect the listener without having to be experienced live or in the company of others.

40 What, according to the text, is the danger of 'an obsessional insistence on perfection' (line 8) when recording music?

....

41 Explain in your own words the underlying reasons why the famous pianist disliked performing at concerts.

....

For me, listening to records has many advantages over concert-going. I choose what I want to hear, when I want to hear it, without having any of the distractions of the concert hall. Even in the case of opera and ballet, the absence of the visual element enables me to appreciate the musical content to a greater degree than would otherwise be possible, and, for this reason, I have often found it helpful to listen to a recording of an opera before I see it for the first time: conversely, when I know an opera well I can visualise the scene as I listen to the recording.

Of course, none of this is to say that a recording can ever completely replace a live performance. The personalities of those taking part and the interaction between the audience and the performers give live performances a character of their own which cannot be reproduced in the studio. Nor can these be retained in recordings of live concerts; indeed all that the latter tends to do is to reveal more clearly the kinds of   **line 12** imperfection one often fails to notice in the concert hall, where one's attention is held by the general momentum of the music. In the last analysis it will always be the live performance which really matters; nevertheless, the satisfaction to be gained from playing records is almost limitless.

42   What allows the writer to have a better appreciation of an opera when listening to it at home rather than a live performance?

   ....

43   Which phrase in the first text echoes the 'kinds of imperfection' (lines 12–13)?

   ....

44   In a paragraph of between **50** and **70** words, summarise **in your own words as far as possible** what advantages, according to the two texts, attending a live concert has over listening to recorded music at home. Write your summary **on the separate answer sheet**.

PAPER 4 LISTENING (40 minutes approximately)

Part 1

You will hear four different extracts. For questions **1–8**, choose the answer (**A**, **B** or **C**) which fits best according to what you hear. There are two questions for each extract.

Extract 1

You hear a lecturer talking about wordplay, that is, using words humorously.

1 How does the speaker feel about wordplay?

  A intrigued
  B delighted
  C amused

1

2 The speaker believes that if people do not share the same sense of humour,

  A they stop telling one another jokes.
  B they start to behave in a more serious way.
  C they are unlikely to get on well.

2

Extract 2

You hear a film director talking about actors recording the voices for animated films.

3 The actors cope well with recording voices for animated films because

  A there are no distractions in the recording studio.
  B the director provides what they need.
  C they have been chosen for their special skills.

3

4 The recording session is video-taped so that

  A the director has a copy to work from.
  B the actors can see themselves.
  C the animators can get ideas for their drawings.

4

Extract 3

You hear part of a radio programme about environmental issues.

5 What concerns the speaker about the environmentalist's views?

    A her lack of evidence
    B criticisms from other experts
    C a contradiction in her argument

6 What are the predictions about?

    A population expansion
    B global warming
    C exploitation of resources

Extract 4

You hear part of an interview with Pauline, a woman footballer.

7 What does Pauline recall about her experience of playing football while at university?

    A Girls were discriminated against on several occasions.
    B A fellow player inspired her to take up the sport.
    C Sporting opportunities were limited.

8 What does Pauline believe will ensure the future of women's football?

    A We need to see women playing a better quality game.
    B People need to consider women's football as a serious job.
    C Women footballers need to develop their future.

Part 2

You will hear part of a radio programme about the sense of hearing. For questions **9–17**, complete the sentences with a word or short phrase.

It's a common

	9

that we all have the same auditory experience.

The sound takes the form of a

	10

as it travels to the inner ear.

Only when a sound reaches the

	11

, do we register that we have heard it.

An Australian biologist is sure that men can identify the

	12

of an animal emitting a sound better than women.

He suggests that this skill evolved when man was primarily a

	13

The biologist thinks that women can hear shrill sounds so that

they can recognise

	14

in a child's cry.

Differences in the hearing of males and females have been detected

immediately after

	15

Some people in Manchester have been disturbed by an irritating noise

similar to a

	16

Every one of the

	17

received has been from women.

Part 3

You will hear a book reviewer on a radio programme about science discussing a book about the human brain. For questions **18–22**, choose the answer (**A**, **B**, **C** or **D**) which fits best according to what you hear.

18   According to Peter Hughes, 'mapping the mind' is a way of enabling scientists to

   A   help people control negative emotions.
   B   explain the basis of human actions.
   C   encourage individuals to become more self aware.
   D   understand how character is fixed at an early age.

   | 18 |

19   The author of the book appears to believe that control of brain activity

   A   will require development of new techniques.
   B   will require the invention of new technology.
   C   is close to being a reality.
   D   is already very precise.

   | 19 |

20   One effect of neuroscience being new is that

   A   neuroscientists have no generally agreed goal.
   B   the media pay particular attention to it.
   C   considerable funding is available.
   D   there are tight government controls.

   | 20 |

21   In the reviewer's opinion, the book should have included

   A   social implications.
   B   the technology that is used.
   C   the nature of consciousness.
   D   interactions within the brain.

   | 21 |

22   The book which is being reviewed seems to be

   A   a guide to a popular subject.
   B   one of the first in its field.
   C   an academic work for specialists.
   D   a simplified introduction.

   | 22 |

Part 4

You will hear part of a radio programme in which two writers, Tanya and Sam, discuss writing. For questions **23–28**, decide whether the opinions are expressed by only one of the speakers, or whether the speakers agree.

Write   **T**   for Tanya
       S   for Sam
or   **B**   for Both, where they agree.

---

23   All writers want to be well known.

     23

24   Writing demands self-confidence.

     24

25   When writers meet, their conversations tend to be very negative.

     25

26   Readers can recognise the superiority of literature over books written by celebrities.

     26

27   The merit of a novel lies in the quality of its ideas.

     27

28   Writers would find it helpful to discuss their work in progress.

     28

PAPER 5   SPEAKING (19 minutes for pairs of candidates, 28 minutes for groups of three)

This test is also suitable for groups of three students; this only occurs at the last test of a session where a centre has an uneven number of candidates.

There are two examiners. One (the Interlocutor) conducts the test, providing you with the necessary materials and explaining what you have to do. The other examiner (the Assessor) will be introduced to you, but then takes no further part in the interaction.

Part 1 (3 minutes for pairs of candidates, 4 minutes for groups of three)

The Interlocutor first asks you and your partner(s) a few questions which focus on information about yourselves and personal opinions.

Part 2 (4 minutes for pairs of candidates, 6 minutes for groups of three)

In this part of the test you and your partner(s) are asked to talk together. The Interlocutor places a single picture or a set of pictures on the table in front of you. This stimulus provides the basis for a discussion. The Interlocutor first asks an introductory question which focuses on one or two of the pictures. After about a minute (or two for groups of three), the Interlocutor gives you both/all a decision-making task based on the same set of pictures.

The picture for Part 2 is on pages C8–C9 of the colour section.

Part 3 (12 minutes for pairs of candidates, 18 minutes for groups of three)

You are each given the opportunity to talk for two minutes, to comment after your partner has spoken and to take part in a more general discussion.

The Interlocutor gives you a card with a question written on it and asks you to talk about it for two minutes. After you have spoken, your partner is first asked to comment and then the Interlocutor asks you both another question related to the topic on the card. This procedure is repeated, so that your partner receives a card and speaks for two minutes, you are given an opportunity to comment and a follow-up question is asked. For a group of three, there is a third card and the procedure is repeated once more.

Finally, the Interlocutor asks some further questions, which leads to a discussion on a general theme related to the subjects already covered in Part 3.

The cards for Part 3 are on pages C10–C12 of the colour section.

Test 1 Key

Paper 1   Reading (1 hour 30 minutes)

Part 1   (one mark for each correct answer)

1 A	2 D	3 C	4 A	5 C	6 B	7 A	8 A	9 A
10 B	11 C	12 D	13 A	14 A	15 B	16 C		
17 D	18 B							

Part 2   (two marks for each correct answer)

19 C	20 B	21 B	22 A	23 A	24 D	25 A	26 B

Part 3   (two marks for each correct answer)

27 F	28 D	29 G	30 H	31 B	32 E	33 A

Part 4   (two marks for each correct answer)

34 C	35 B	36 D	37 A	38 B	39 D	40 D

Paper 2   Writing (2 hours)

Task-specific mark schemes

Question 1
Content
Major points:
The expression of views on the given areas:
• transporting children to school
• loss of trade in town centre
• poor and expensive public transport
Inclusion of possible solutions to the problems above.

Further points:
Any ideas relevant to the discussion of pollution, traffic and accidents and any possible solutions to people's concerns, e.g.
• an analysis of why people use their cars so much
• advertising to show dangers of cars and alternative means of transport

Range
Language for expressing and supporting views, and for making recommendations.

Appropriacy of register and format
Appropriate format for a proposal, e.g. clear introduction with possible use of headings.

Organisation and cohesion
Organisation of content into sections. Ideas organised and argument well structured. Adequate use of linking and paragraphing.

Target reader
The local council would understand the writer's viewpoint.

Question 2
Content
Description of two or more achievements they consider important (e.g. living independently, travelling). Personal anecdote is appropriate but the importance of the achievement must be made clear.

Range
Language of description, narrative and analysis.

Appropriacy of register and format
Register and format appropriate for an article in a magazine, possibly with use of section headings.

Organisation and cohesion
Clear development of description and analysis. Adequate use of linking and paragraphing.

Target reader
Would be interested in the article and encouraged to consider what is most important in life.

Question 3
Content
Description of how they learnt about the value of money, e.g. pocket money, small jobs.
Importance of money in relation to other things in life.

Range
Language of description, narrative and discussion.

Appropriacy of register and format
Register and format appropriate for a letter to a newspaper. Register must be consistent.

Organisation and cohesion
Early reference to reason for writing. Clear organisation of points. Adequate use of linking and paragraphing.

Target reader
'Family Page' editor/readers would have a clear idea of the writer's experience and viewpoint.

Question 4

Content
Description of the visit to the historical building or site.
Evaluation of the visit and how such visits can encourage the study of history.

Range
Language of description, narration and persuasion.

Appropriacy of register and format
Register and format appropriate for a report for a magazine, possibly including section headings. Register must be consistent.

Organisation and cohesion
Clear organisation of content with adequate use of linking and paragraphing.

Target reader
Would be well informed about the visit to the building/site.
Would understand the view expressed about history/the past.

Question 5(a)

Content
Clear reference to the book chosen.
Brief summary of the theme of the book, leading to an analysis of Macon's relationship with his brother and sister and how and why it changes.

Range
Language of description, narration and evaluation.

Appropriacy of register and format
Review with register and format appropriate to an arts magazine. Register must be consistent throughout.

Organisation and cohesion
Clear development from introduction to development of the main focus, leading to a clear conclusion.

Target reader
Would be informed about the book and know something about Macon's relationship with his brother and sister and how and why it changes.

Question 5(b)

Content
Clear reference to the book chosen.
Description of storyline elements relevant to the theme of survival, and an evaluation of how the survivors deal with their situation.

Range
Language of description, narration and evaluation.

Appropriacy of register and format
Neutral article.

Organisation and cohesion
Clear presentation and development of ideas. Appropriate linking and paragraphing. Clear conclusion.

Target reader
Would be informed about the theme of survival in the book and understand the writer's viewpoint.

Question 5(c)

Content
Clear reference to the book chosen.
Clear reference to the events, characters and relationships in the novel, and some comment on the qualities of good literature.

Range
Language of description, narration and persuasion.

Appropriacy of register and format
Formal register and format consistent and appropriate for a letter to a literary magazine.

Organisation and cohesion
Clear presentation and development of the three areas under consideration, with appropriate linking and paragraphing. Clear conclusion.

Target reader
Would have an understanding of the nature and purpose of the novel, and the qualities that make it more than just a spy story.

Paper 3   Use of English (1 hour 30 minutes)

Part 1   (one mark for each correct answer)
1 up   2 whose   3 whatever/what   4 fact   5 Like/like
6 could/would   7 out   8 with   9 Should/should
10 somewhere/anywhere   11 few   12 little   13 means/way
14 have   15 us

Part 2   (one mark for each correct answer)
16 recognisable/recognizable   17 ripens   18 maturity   19 extensively
20 unknown   21 suppliers   22 competitors   23 consequently
24 emergence   25 threatening

Part 3   (two marks for each correct answer)
26 view   27 serious   28 bear   29 clear   30 running   31 badly

Part 4 (one mark for each correct section)

32 has/includes/contains/gives/is (1) + a vivid account of (1)
33 is prone to (1) + attack/getting attacked/being attacked (1)
34 cast/shed/throw (1) + some/any light on how (1)
35 come to terms (1) + with the fact that (1)
36 took me aback / by surprise (1) + when/that you began OR to hear/see you OR hearing/seeing you (1)
37 not take Janice long (1) + to get over / to get rid of (1) OR not take long for Janice (1) + to get over (1)
38 until the storm (had) subsided that (1) + the extent (1)
39 to dawn (1) + on Alan (1)

Part 5 (questions 40–43 two marks for each correct answer)

40 A viewer may be mystified/confused/puzzled/surprised/amazed.
41 The painting reminds them of something negative/bad.
42 high prices / lots of advance orders
43 'too quickly for the taste of' the surlier culture critics
44 (one mark for each content point, up to ten marks for summary skills)
   The paragraph should include the following points:
   i   may evoke pleasant memories
   ii reproduce real beauty (e.g. natural world)
   iii are a status symbol in modern society
   iv now seen as a commodity / financial investment / valuable possession

Paper 4   Listening (40 minutes approximately)

Part 1 (one mark for each correct answer)
1 C   2 A   3 A   4 B   5 B   6 A   7 C   8 A

Part 2 (one mark for each correct answer)
9 luxury   10 chemical composition   11 (heavy-duty) rollers
12 after(-)taste   13 self(-)medication   14 (the) blood pressure
15 (the/our) mood(s)/emotion(s)   16 guilt   17 treat mentality

Part 3 (one mark for each correct answer)
18 D   19 A   20 D   21 B   22 C

Part 4 (one mark for each correct answer)
23 B   24 D   25 B   26 H   27 B   28 D

Transcript

Certificate of Proficiency in English Listening Test. Test 1.

I'm going to give you the instructions for this test.

I'll introduce each part of the test and give you time to look at the questions.

At the start of each piece you'll hear this sound:

tone

You'll hear each piece twice.

Remember, while you're listening, write your answers on the question paper.

You'll have five minutes at the end of the test to copy your answers onto the separate answer sheet.

There will now be a pause. Please ask any questions now, because you must not speak during the test.

[pause]

PART 1

Now open your question paper and look at Part One.

[pause]

You'll hear four different extracts. For questions 1 to 8, choose the answer (A, B or C) which fits best according to what you hear. There are two questions for each extract.

Extract 1

[pause]

tone

Presenter: It's certainly not that Nunan is untalented. In his earlier films, *Lives at Sea* for example, produced, when? 20 years ago and – one of my favourites – it would have been a much poorer film without the incidental music. The spectacular set pieces would have suffered from being over long. As it is, we are swept from mood to mood, changing from passion to serenity in one scene. And why this was so important was that it actually gave new layers of understanding to the viewer. We wouldn't have got it otherwise. So *I* was his fiercest defender, as you may well remember, because *Lives at Sea* was so controversial that I felt that it *needed* defending; and Nunan's work particularly so. And then other films started to come out and the suspicion began to creep up on me that he had one eye firmly on sales, which then became both eyes and that's when a very good composer was lost to us.

[pause]

tone

[The recording is repeated.]

[pause]

Extract 2   [pause]

tone

Presenter: The international authority on the anthropology of shopping is Paco Underhill. Paco, how did you become an anthropologist of shopping?

Paco: Well, I was an urban geographer, and it occurred to me that the same tools that I'd been using to look at what made a good street or the dynamics of a bus stop I could use to see what makes a good store.

Presenter: Tell me a bit about the methodology.

Paco: We've basically taken the tools of anthropology and simply applied them to your local store. We collect information in a variety of different ways. For example, we assign what we call trackers to a store, which is somebody who just chooses a customer randomly as they enter an aisle or doorway, and simply observes them through their shopping process. Their instructions are simply to look, and if they feel that they're making the person uncomfortable, to just abandon that one and go find somebody else. At the same time we are following people, we have video cameras filming. There is no piece of behaviour too small for our cameras or trackers to record.

[pause]

tone

[The recording is repeated.]

[pause]

Extract 3   [pause]

tone

Interviewer: Anthony, have you any advice for people who have some money to invest, buying stocks and shares, that sort of thing?

Anthony: Well yes, I think there would be a few things I would highlight. I think going against the trend is a good way to invest. Of course, not everyone can do this. Some people like the comfort they get from doing what everyone else is doing. And also I think I would recommend, generally, not to worry about timing, as it's a very difficult thing to know exactly when to buy and sell your shares, and get it right every time. And another thing, they shouldn't just buy on tips or whatever, they should really try and understand the business, the underlying business, you know. And well, finally, I'd suggest that if there is an area that someone has had experience in, for example, if they'd been a doctor and knew about medicine, perhaps they should concentrate their investments in that area, because then they'll have a bit of a competitive edge on the mass of investors who don't have such specialist knowledge.

[pause]

tone

[The recording is repeated.]

[pause]

Extract 4   [pause]

                       tone

Presenter: My guest today is Irene Donovan, who leads the all-woman band she formed
             50 years ago, which still carries her name, and she's just brought out a book to
             celebrate that auspicious anniversary. Irene, the band isn't a unique phenomenon,
             is it?

Irene: We're certainly not a one-off, or even the first. But, you know, people come up to
             me and say 'I saw you play in Jamaica,' or wherever, and I've never been there in
             my life. You see, mine is the only name people remember.

Presenter: You haven't let up on your gruelling programme of tours?

Irene: No, I'm still going strong, touch wood.

Presenter: Now when it all started, so long ago, how did the bandleaders then react to an
             all-woman band? It must have been quite unusual.

Irene: Well they more or less accepted it with a sort of snigger really, they thought, oh
             well, it's a bit ropey, won't be long before it folds, won't affect us. But I was
             determined to make the grade if I possibly could, and I was able to put together
             some pretty strong musicians.

Presenter: And you've always kept up a high standard, haven't you?

                       [pause]

                       tone

                       [The recording is repeated.]

                       That's the end of Part One.

                       Now turn to Part Two.

PART 2   [pause]

                       *You'll hear part of a radio programme about chocolate. For questions 9 to
                       17, complete the sentences with a word or short phrase.*

                       You now have forty-five seconds in which to look at Part Two.

                       [pause]

                       tone

Presenter: When it was introduced to London in the mid-seventeenth century, a pound of
             chocolate cost the equivalent of £500, and by the eighteenth century this
             quintessentially blameless bedtime drink was seen as the height of indulgence.
             So, what exactly is it about chocolate that has taken it from luxury to near-
             universal pleasure? Dr Peter Barham of the Physics department at Bristol
             University has been trying to find out. He analysed the physics and chemistry of
             chocolate from pod to bar, and discovered what it is that makes it so appealing.
                 The reasons for cravings for chocolate lie in its chemical composition.
             Chocolate, like coffee, contains caffeine, but according to Dr Barham the main
             stimulant is another chemical, the name of which comes from the Latin for the
             cocoa tree.

The reason why chocolate feels so good when we eat it is because of its particle size, Dr Barham says. Particle size, apparently, imparts that familiar rich, creamy texture. And it is this richness that advertising copywriters use to market chocolate as a sensuous pleasure. During the manufacture of chocolate, the liquid mixture is crunched through heavy-duty rollers. This reduces the particles of solid ingredients in the chocolate to microscopic size. And the smaller the particles, the better the emulsion – the liquid with tiny solid particles suspended in it. Basically, the smaller the particles, the thicker the emulsion, which is important if you like chocolate to linger in the mouth and give a pleasing after-taste.

Another person investigating the subject is Professor David Warburton, head of the Psychopharmacology department of Reading University. According to his research, chocolate increases feelings of well-being; indeed, eating too much chocolate may be a form of self-medication. Professor Warburton found that more than fifty per cent of people who eat four squares of chocolate feel in a better frame of mind afterwards. This is thought to be because chocolate contains a molecule which is closely related to amphetamines. This raises blood pressure and boosts glucose levels, making people feel more alert and giving a sense of well-being. Over-indulging on chocolate may, in fact, be an attempt to regulate the chemicals that control mood after an emotionally upsetting incident.

Chocolate addiction has been studied by doctors Marion Hetherington and Jennifer Macdiarmid from the University of Dundee. They have found that although eating chocolate made people feel better, in genuine addicts the pleasure was short-lived. Most felt incredibly guilty after a chocolate binge. And this guilt may do them even more harm since guilt creates stress hormones, which mobilise fatty acids such as cholesterol and cholesterol clogs up arteries, which, as we all know, can lead to certain illnesses.

According to psychologist Corinne Sweet, we have what's called a 'treat mentality', which means we can become emotionally addicted to chocolate. We are hooked on rewarding ourselves for 'good behaviour', but these treats are ultimately bad for us. Rewards, convenience food, comfort food – however we view chocolate, we need to recognise that chocolate is not really a healthy food option.

[pause]

Now you'll hear Part Two again.

tone

[The recording is repeated.]

[pause]

That's the end of Part Two.

Now turn to Part Three.

[pause]

PART 3   *You'll hear an interview with Derek Allen, an author, about the writing process. For questions 18 to 22, choose the answer (A, B, C or D) which fits best according to what you hear.*

You now have one minute in which to look at Part Three.

[pause]

tone

Interviewer: ... OK, and now we move to our section on books and authors. The book we're discussing today is *Travelling in Space* and we'll be discussing it with its creator, Derek Allen. It was originally presented as a 12-part radio series and it's a pretty outrageous and satirical science fiction epic but offers a gleefully pessimistic view of modern society. A year later, the book of the radio programme was published and it went straight to the top of the best-seller list – it sold 10,000 copies in the first month alone. Derek Allen, welcome. Now, can I start by asking you what is the essence of its success?

Derek Allen: Of course, it's an unanswerable question. If one knew the answer, one could bottle it. The only thing I can say with any degree of certainty is that, however extraordinary its success may have turned out to be, there's a little bit of me that isn't surprised because I actually know how much I put into it in terms of worry and stress. I mean, we all know the packaging can be very attractive but it's what's inside that matters. And, you see, there's a little bit of me that doesn't expect anything I've written to be any good, so you work at it a bit more and a bit more, and you are so determined to pack everything in, so it doesn't surprise me that people have got so much out of it in the end.

Interviewer: It's a funny thing, isn't it, radio and writing books go together, don't they?

Derek Allen: The overlap between radio listeners and a book audience is absolutely enormous, very much more so than between a book audience and television. But it is words. Now the thing is that one of the strengths of the book is that I originally wrote it all as dialogue. Now the thing about that is that the characters, therefore, are forced to tell the story. So the range of dialogue the characters have to employ is enormous. The mere fact of getting the characters always having to be the ones who tell the story, that gives you a tremendously good backbone for then writing a book.

Interviewer: Absolutely. Now, the thing that strikes me is that in some ways you are 'sending up' the craft of science fiction and yet you've become a hero of the genre. Curious, isn't it?

Derek Allen: As far as I was concerned, I wasn't 'sending up' science fiction. I was using science fiction as a vehicle for 'sending up' everything else. In comedy, for example, a sketch can create some sort of surreal premise on which a universe is based that will then last for two or three minutes and then you're on to the next scene. And I always wanted to say – but what are the consequences of that surreal premise? So, for example, right back at the beginning of the story, it could start with a man whose house is demolished to make way for a by-pass and so it then becomes conceivable that the earth then gets demolished to make way for a hyper-space by-pass. OK, now let's move it on again, let's give that consequences and of course, once you've blown up the earth, you are kind of committed to science fiction!

Interviewer:	Yes, and the other thing I notice is that while most writers avoid situations based on coincidence, you positively revel in it.
Derek Allen:	Yes, well, coincidence is the thing that for many authors indicates that the plot has broken down and he is in danger of losing the reader! But I decided to embrace coincidences. As a coincidence is difficult to write about and to do it successfully you have to understand the force that you're dealing with. For example, I can put characters in great jeopardy and you have a dilemma, which is, that if the jeopardy is going to mean anything, then you can't get them out of it with one bound. So it's got to be something, something that's going to be of equal weight. I was watching a TV programme on judo where the principle is to use your opponent's weight against himself. So every problem I come up with has to be resolved by something that is equally implausible!
Interviewer:	So is this all clearly delineated for you before you start?
Derek Allen:	Well, no, normally what an artist would do is rough out the general shape of the picture – a man's going to be standing here, there's going to be a donkey over here or whatever and you've got the main shape of the picture. Then you gradually put in a background – you rough it out in grey and then you put in the layers of paint but the first thing that's there is the shape of it.
	Now, if *I* was a painter, I would start painting in enormous detail down in the bottom left-hand corner and by the time I got to the top, everything would be out of scale.
Interviewer:	Right, OK well, let's bring in our guest reviewer now …

[pause]

Now you'll hear Part Three again.

tone

[The recording is repeated.]

[pause]

That's the end of Part Three.

Now turn to Part Four.

PART 4

[pause]

You'll hear two travel agents talking about the rise in popularity of adventure holidays. For questions 23 to 28, decide whether the opinions are expressed by only one of the speakers, or whether the speakers agree. Write D for Daniel, H for Helena, or B for both, where they agree.

You now have thirty seconds in which to look at Part Four.

[pause]

tone

Daniel:	What did you think of the talk, Helena? – the one given by the woman from Breakout Travel.
Helena:	Yeah, interesting stuff. So, adrenaline adventure trips are what we'll be selling more of in the next few years.
Daniel:	Mm. I liked the phrase she coined. What was it? The fear-good factor. So apparently what people are craving now are white-knuckle journeys of derring-do.

Helena:	I've noticed how people who are trying out this adventure-style travel are coming back for more. Once they've tried whale watching, chasing tornadoes or hammering along white water rapids on a raft, they're quite simply hooked.
Daniel:	There does seem to be a real lure to this type of travel – they can't keep away.
Helena:	It does strike me that more and more people are choosing to take their lives into their own hands when they go on holiday.
Daniel:	I suppose come the annual holiday some people go looking for the ultimate challenge. I guess it's a way out if you're stuck in a rut, feeling fed up with a humdrum existence.
Helena:	I felt totally exhausted just hearing about some of the trips Breakout organise.
Daniel:	Yeah, can you imagine spending your long-earned, two weeks off like that?
Helena:	You'd get to the end of the day completely done in because your adrenaline levels have rocketed. Come to think of it though, I'd give it a go. Like the white water rafting …
Daniel:	What, where you're paddling along in your raft very happily, thinking you're comfortable and the next second being plunged into freezing cold water. I wouldn't find that thrilling.
Helena:	But that's just it. You'd be absolutely in it, in the thick of that element, with no way to ever remove yourself from it – that must be the real high of it.
Daniel:	Well, anyway, it doesn't matter what I think. If my customers come in wanting thrills and spills, it's up to me to sell them something that'll live up to their expectations.
Helena:	I wonder what it'll mean for all the 'sun 'n' sea' type holidays we sell in their thousands every year? I mean, with people wanting something more adventurous, lying in the sun is no longer enough, especially taking into account the ease of …
Daniel:	… discovering uncharted rivers or sailing across the Atlantic in a leather boat. (*laughs*) Easy, I don't think so.
Helena:	Ease of availability and affordability, I was going to say! For our parents' generation going on a package tour to wherever was the pinnacle of excitement. It must have been mould-breaking then, but now things have moved on.
Daniel:	We were brought up doing that every year, thinking there must be something else, something more and everyone must have felt the same. And maybe adventure travel is it.
Helena:	Don't you think though, these holidays are really only for dare-devils, whatever your views on green issues. I mean, there is such a thing as your own personal challenge level.
Daniel:	I'd never go climbing ice cliffs myself. But even with no previous experience, if you have enough determination to get the hang of new skills, surely nothing will stop you.
Helena:	What surprises me is this family aspect of adventure travel which is on the increase.
Daniel:	Mm, like the example quoted of the family who went to northern Thailand …

[pause]

Now you'll hear Part Four again.

tone

[The recording is repeated.]

[pause]

That's the end of Part Four.

There'll now be a pause of five minutes for you to copy your answers onto the separate answer sheet. Be sure to follow the numbering of all the questions. I'll remind you when there is one minute left, so that you're sure to finish in time.

[pause]

You have one more minute left.

[pause]

That's the end of the test. Please stop now.

Test 2 Key

Paper 1   Reading (1 hour 30 minutes)

Part 1   (one mark for each correct answer)

1 B	2 A	3 C	4 D	5 B	6 A	7 B	8 B	9 C
10 C	11 A	12 D	13 A	14 D	15 B	16 A		
17 A	18 D							

Part 2   (two marks for each correct answer)

19 A	20 C	21 A	22 C	23 C	24 B	25 A	26 B

Part 3   (two marks for each correct answer)

27 C	28 H	29 E	30 G	31 D	32 A	33 F

Part 4   (two marks for each correct answer)

34 C	35 B	36 A	37 B	38 D	39 C	40 D

Paper 2   Writing (2 hours)

Task-specific mark schemes

Question 1
Content
Major points:
The role of computers in education, and their impact on:
- the classroom
- teachers
- learning

The writer's own viewpoint on the matter.

Further points:
Any other points relevant to the discussion.

Range
Language for expressing and supporting opinions, and for reaching conclusions.

Appropriacy of register and format
Formal essay-type register. Register appropriate to the writer's role as a student.

Organisation and cohesion
Clear organisation of points with adequate use of paragraphing. Logical development of argument and clear conclusion(s).

Target reader
Would have a clear understanding of the writer's viewpoint.

Question 2

Content
Description of present leisure and sports facilities.
Evaluation of their use and quality.
Recommendations for improving and extending facilities.

Range
Language of description, analysing, evaluating and making recommendations.

Appropriacy of register and format
Register and format appropriate for that of a proposal, possibly with relevant section headings. Register can be formal or neutral in tone, but must be consistent.

Organisation and cohesion
Presentation of ideas and information should be well structured and organised into sections. Adequate use of linking and paragraphing.

Target reader
Would be informed of level and quality of present facilities for young people.
Would understand what recommendations are being made.

Question 3

Content
Description of the interior of the restaurant.
Description of the food and service.
Evaluation of the restaurant and clear recommendation.

Range
Language of description, evaluation and recommendation.

Appropriacy of register and format
Formal/informal register and format appropriate for a review. Register must be consistent.

Organisation and cohesion
Clear development of ideas with adequate use of linking and paragraphing, and possible use of headings.

Target reader
Would be informed about the restaurant and the experience.
Would be able to decide whether or not the restaurant is to be recommended.

Question 4

Content
The letter should provide appropriate information about the chosen individual; a significant proportion of the letter should be devoted to reasons why the individual should win the title; it should evaluate the significance of the individual's contribution over the past ten years.

Range
Language of description, analysis, persuasion and recommendation.

Appropriacy of register and format
Register and format appropriate for a letter to a radio programme. Register can be formal/informal but must be consistent.

Organisation and cohesion
Well-structured argument, which can be either a clear division between information and the evaluation of the individual or an integrated approach in which the person is simultaneously described and evaluated.
Adequate use of linking and paragraphing. A clear conclusion is necessary.

Target reader
Should be informed about the person and persuaded of the significant contribution they have made to society.

Question 5(a)

Content
Clear reference to the book chosen.
Description and comparison of the Leary household and Muriel's home in Singleton Street, and analysis of how Macon adapts to each one.

Range
Language of description, comparison and analysis.

Appropriacy of register and format
Neutral article.

Organisation and cohesion
Clear presentation and development of ideas. Appropriate linking and paragraphing. Clear conclusion.

Target reader
Would understand the writer's viewpoint.

Question 5(b)

Content
Clear reference to the book chosen.
Reasons for popularity of science fiction, e.g. elements of horror, treatment of topical issues.
Description of storyline and the Triffids, and how the characters respond to fear of the unknown.

Range
Language of description, narration, persuasion and evaluation.

Appropriacy of register and format
Formal letter appropriate for the Arts Page of a newspaper. Register must be consistent throughout.

Organisation and cohesion
Clear presentation and development of ideas with appropriate linking of
paragraphs from the introduction to the main body of the letter. Clear conclusion.

Target reader
Would be clear about why the book would make a good film.

Question 5(c)

Content
Clear reference to the book chosen.
Clear identification of Segura's role with reference to his behaviour and actions
when dealing with other characters.
Comparison of villainous and redeeming features of his character.

Range
Language of description, narration, comparison and evaluation.

Appropriacy of register and format
Article appropriate for magazine.

Organisation and cohesion
Clear presentation and development of ideas. Appropriate linking and
paragraphing. Clear conclusion.

Target reader
Would have a balanced and rounded view of Segura's character.

Paper 3   Use of English (1 hour 30 minutes)

Part 1   (one mark for each correct answer)
1 itself   2 though/when/if   3 few   4 than   5 Apart/apart
6 many   7 make/scrape   8 at   9 place/hold/root   10 up
11 Despite/despite   12 capable   13 this/that   14 in   15 such

Part 2   (one mark for each correct answer)
16 disapproval   17 appreciably   18 unwise   19 modification(s)
20 ambiguity   21 undergoing   22 infrequent   23 noticeable
24 maintenance   25 effective

Part 3   (two marks for each correct answer)
26 influence   27 sensitive   28 dedicated   29 line   30 concern
31 confidence

Part 4   (one mark for each correct section)
32 is restricted to (1) + those in / those passengers in / passengers in (1)
33 no circumstances (1) + should/must this door be / should/must you leave this
   door / is this door to be (1)

34 were (always) a (constant/continual) source (1) + of (continual) embarrassment to (1)
35 prospects are there / are the prospects (1) + of the new venture's/venture getting (1) OR prospects does the new venture (1) + have of getting (1)
36 take much / take a lot of (1) + notice of (1)
37 far as Colin (1) + is/'s concerned (1)
38 took (1) + exception to (1)
39 in the dark (1) + for her own (1)

Part 5   (questions 40–43 two marks for each correct answer)

40 It is a metaphor of hunting applied to the modern world.
41 (Because since eating grass all day long is a monotonous activity) the herbivores' descendants would be adapted to a monotonous existence.
42 Seeing only what we want to.
43 By not interacting with fellow city dwellers we avoid overloading ourselves and others with unnecessary stimuli.
44 (one mark for each content point, up to ten marks for summary skills)
The paragraph should include the following points:
  i Some people (e.g. businessmen) find stimulus in work.
  ii Some people with boring jobs have fascinating hobbies.
  iii Stimuli of modern life can lead to quicker reactions.
  iv Too many stimuli can lead to people switching off and ignoring them / adopting new rules of behaviour.

Paper 4   Listening (40 minutes approximately)

Part 1   (one mark for each correct answer)
1 C   **2** B   **3** C   **4** B   **5** C   **6** B   **7** B   **8** C

Part 2   (one mark for each correct answer)
9 (obstacle) course   **10** blood   **11** (the very nature of) intelligence
12 (small) brains   **13** dustbin   **14** video camera / camcorder
15 (the) training/teaching (of) (a) dog(s)/animal(s)   **16** shorthand
17 vacuum cleaner

Part 3   (one mark for each correct answer)
18 D   **19** A   **20** C   **21** B   **22** C

Part 4   (one mark for each correct answer)
23 D   **24** B   **25** K   **26** B   **27** K   **28** D

Transcript   *Certificate of Proficiency in English Listening Test. Test 2.*

I'm going to give you the instructions for this test.

I'll introduce each part of the test and give you time to look at the questions.

At the start of each piece you'll hear this sound:

tone

You'll hear each piece twice.

Remember, while you're listening, write your answers on the question paper.

You'll have five minutes at the end of the test to copy your answers onto the separate answer sheet.

There will now be a pause. Please ask any questions now, because you must not speak during the test.

[pause]

Now open your question paper and look at Part One.

[pause]

PART 1   *You'll hear four different extracts. For questions 1 to 8, choose the answer (A, B or C) which fits best according to what you hear. There are two questions for each extract.*

Extract 1   [pause]

tone

Presenter:	I'm standing in Wicksteed Park with its managing director, Ray Taylor. Ray, Wicksteed is a very successful amusement park, isn't it?
Ray:	It certainly is, and it's the largest *free* playground in Europe, with rides that go from ones for kiddies and their grandparents to white-knuckle rides for the aficionado who doesn't mind screaming and getting their stomach turned upside down, the ones I only go on once and never again.
Presenter:	And how did it all start?
Ray:	It was developed from about 1916 as the dream of Charles Wicksteed, who founded and ran a local engineering works, and wanted to do something for the local community.
Presenter:	He was also an inventor, wasn't he?
Ray:	That's right, it was a hobby he was passionate about. He was responsible for several of our rides, and about 1925 he invented this amazing-looking contraption, which is the world's first bread cutting and buttering machine, for the five thousand teas that had to be prepared every day. It had a tremendous output – 2500 slices an hour, and every piece a winner.

[pause]

tone

[The recording is repeated.]

[pause]

Extract 2   [pause]

tone

Speaker: I vividly remember standing secretly on the top flight of the stairs at home, listening up through the hatch in the ceiling into the loft, where my father, who was an amateur radio enthusiast, would sit endlessly until two or three in the morning sending and receiving messages on his radio transmitter. I didn't know who the strange voices belonged to, but it was a magic discovery for me. There was life beyond the small provincial town I lived in and it gave me an insatiable appetite to taste it.

My first job on leaving school was delivering televisions. I was also pursuing, what was for me, very much a passion, trying to be in a pop group, write songs and make records and things. One afternoon in 1978, I was driving around the centre of town and suddenly on Radio 1, came my record. It was the most traumatic moment of my life. It was the most overwhelming thing to realise that something that we had done, that started out as a couple of kids making noises in a spare bedroom at home, was suddenly now on national radio.

[pause]

tone

[The recording is repeated.]

[pause]

Extract 3   [pause]

tone

Presenter: Tonight's Front Row takes us to the heart of theatreland, the Great White Way, Broadway, and we talk to the multi-faceted Joachim Rowntree, ex film actor and acerbic theatre critic of the magazine *Village Voice* but very much in the news at the moment with the success of his directorial debut *The Papermaker* – the story of an ageing actor finding himself on a retreat in the backwoods – and breaking box-office records since its recent opening. Tonight in yet another new role, that of theatre historian, Rowntree explores the genre of theatrical works of self-discovery, similar to *The Papermaker*, discussing their role as the conscience of Broadway.

Joachim Rowntree: I think I've tried it all in theatre now, except perhaps coming up with the actual script, but I'm getting too old for that now and I want time away from the bustle of theatres to think and read about my craft, take stock and I think I maybe do have something to say because I have tried my hand at so much …

Presenter: That's Front Row, tonight at 7.15, with Joachim Rowntree.

[pause]

tone

[The recording is repeated.]

[pause]

Extract 4   [pause]

tone

Speaker: Well, an important development in giving a brand name to a new product was PROKAZ, and the role of the name was to establish very quickly the product as something that would become associated with a particular emotional experience, and that was it makes you feel better.

So I began to look at common word parts across many languages that would communicate the main benefits of the product, and one of those was, you know, positive, feelings. Now I realised that 'PRO' was a prefix that worked in many languages that had connotations and suggestions of positivity, something positive.

Then, I also wanted the word to sound modern and scientific, and letters like Z weren't used very much in brand names at this time. So I looked at Zs and I looked at Xs and I looked at Ks, and I began to realise that there were certain sounds that sounded modern and also gave the idea of something dynamic and forward moving, and that's how I got to 'KAZ'. And the word PROKAZ is now actually in popular use, so you could argue that a totally new word was invented.

[pause]

tone

[The recording is repeated.]

[pause]

That's the end of Part One.

Now turn to Part Two.

[pause]

PART 2   *You'll hear the beginning of an interview in which a university professor talks about the robot he has designed, called Jeremy. For questions 9 to 17, complete the sentences with a word or short phrase.*

You now have forty-five seconds in which to look at Part Two.

[pause]

tone

Interviewer: Professor John Shepherd is the inventor of Jeremy, a rather remarkable robot, who has just completed some significant trials. Professor Shepherd, how did Jeremy get on?

Prof. Shepherd: Well, he came through with flying colours. He showed that he can whistle while he works, and that he can negotiate a pretty demanding obstacle course without bumping into anything.

Interviewer:	Tell me, what's the point of robots like this?
Prof. Shepherd:	There are two major reasons for constructing robots. One is quite practical: to build useful devices. Robots are now common in medical laboratories, for instance, to handle potentially hazardous materials, such as blood. In factories they make cars. They can carry out repetitive tasks for long periods accurately, whereas boredom causes people to make mistakes. And they aren't affected by working conditions that we would find intolerable. There's also a growing demand from the general public for robots for the home, both to take over household chores – polishing, perhaps – and as what you might call gimmicks – the robot as butler or pet dog.
Interviewer:	And the other reason for making them?
Prof. Shepherd:	Well, fun though it would be to have robots around the house, this is really by way of being a by-product of a more important and challenging goal. You see, through constructing robots we're trying to gain insight into the very nature of intelligence. At first, researchers tried to make robots intelligent, loading them with complicated computer programmes. But that didn't really work, because the real world is simply *too* complex and changeable. Then we considered ants, which are very successful at what they have to do, even though they don't have large brains. And we thought, maybe we should design something simpler – robots that do just a few tasks. In effect we've moved from trying to make them second-rate human beings to making them particularly sophisticated machines.
Interviewer:	And does Jeremy look like a mechanical man, as in all the films?
Prof. Shepherd:	Far from it. He's just over a metre tall, and is actually more like a dustbin that can trundle around than anything else – big, round and black. He has his own computer on board, and he's got sensors around his middle, which transmit pulses of sound to detect any obstacles in his environment. And where you'd expect his lid, he's got a video camera. All this input goes into the computer, which stops him bumping into things.
Interviewer:	And can he learn from experience, like humans?
Prof. Shepherd:	That's one thing we're interested in studying. We have to put him in the same situation a number of times and get him to choose a behaviour each time. If he picks the right one, he gets a sort of reward, and if he picks the wrong one he's punished. It's very much like training a dog.
Interviewer:	It sounds very human actually, all this talk of reward and punishment. Surely you can't talk about robots in the same way as you would talk about a person, because well they don't have feelings, do they?
Prof. Shepherd:	No. No, no, no, they certainly don't, and we simply use that vocabulary as a sort of shorthand. Of course notions like reward and punishment are misleading, because they rather suggest consciousness, which I'm sure that no one working with computers thinks they have. It'd be better to use terms like 'reinforce' and 'inhibit', which mean more or less the same, but have different connotations. The trouble is they're less accessible to the general public.
Interviewer:	So how close *are* we to robots that can do the housework?
Prof. Shepherd:	Oh, we've still got a long way to go. There *is* a kind of vacuum cleaner that you can leave to get on with the job, but of course the trouble is that it doesn't know what you want to throw away and what you don't.
Interviewer:	Professor Shepherd, thank you.
Prof. Shepherd:	Thank you.

[pause]

Now you'll hear Part Two again.

tone

[The recording is repeated.]

[pause]

That's the end of Part Two.

Now turn to Part Three.

[pause]

PART 3   *You will hear an interview with Dr Janet Thompson who spent many years in Africa, observing chimpanzees. For questions 18 to 22, choose the answer (A, B, C or D) which fits best according to what you hear.*

You now have one minute in which to look at Part Three.

[pause]

tone

Interviewer: Dr Janet Thompson, you made some ground-breaking discoveries about chimpanzees when you lived with and observed them all those years in Africa. For example, you were the first to discover, weren't you, that they use tools, like humans?

Dr Thompson: Yes, humans were considered to be the only tool-using species. And I wasn't looking for anything different. I was just living there in Gombe and observing the chimpanzees all day every day. And then one day, when I was following one of the males, I struggled through a prickly sort of thicket, and found him in a clearing. I saw he was, very intently, using a long blade of grass to poke into a termite's nest, to make it easier for him to get the termites out and eat them. I watched him doing that several times over the next few days before I realized the significance of it. Chimpanzees use tools for all sorts of things. Like us, really.

Interviewer: How dangerous has it got on occasions? You must have been frightened of leopards and lions, for example?

Dr Thompson: Well, the leopards and other things, when I first got to Gombe, you know, I could hear them when I was sleeping out at night but I thought, oh well, and I'd just pull my little blanket over my head and try to ignore them. They are not really that dangerous. Usually if they hear you coming, they get out of the way. Of course, the chimpanzees in the early days, when they lost their fear, they became rather belligerent. But, in fact, they never have really attacked us.

Interviewer: Pretty dangerous though, and yet you brought up a child in this environment. Brave or foolhardy? Which is it?

Dr Thompson: Neither, because Grant was brought up in Gombe when it was really idyllic. There was – well, danger from the chimpanzees, we had to watch him, but the beach, he could swim like a little fish in the lake – it's clean, pure water. You had to make sure he didn't get attacked by lions and things, but it was so free from pollution. And he *liked* being the only little one around. He could get malaria, but you know, think of the worries in the city today.

Interviewer:	Now tell me about father chimpanzees. They don't subscribe much to the family set-up, do they?
Dr Thompson:	They play a very important role actually. They have to protect the territory for the females and young, from incursion by other males. We now know they patrol and defend the boundaries, or even enlarge them and get more resources for their own females and young. It also turns out that males can, when occasion demands, show really good paternal behaviour and care for orphans. We've seen it several times.
Interviewer:	When you realised you had to leave Gombe, to tell the world about the chimpanzees' declining numbers, you left your paradise. But now you do all the things that are the antithesis of that paradise, travelling and being surrounded by people, crowds everywhere. How can you bear it when you enjoyed all those years of peace?
Dr Thompson:	I think it's because I feel it's a mission, and I have to do it. And you know, I had all those years. How many people are lucky enough to live their dream for so long, to be in paradise? Life goes through phases and I just suddenly knew that the next phase was to begin. Once you know you're supposed to be doing something else, you're not happy in paradise any more. You know, you can't change fate.
Interviewer:	You remain nevertheless incredibly optimistic about it all though, don't you? Why?

[pause]

Now you'll hear Part Three again.

tone

[The recording is repeated.]

[pause]

That's the end of Part Three.

Now turn to Part Four.

[pause]

PART 4   *You'll hear two friends, Kathy and Derek, talking about films based on 19th-century novels. For questions 23 to 28, decide whether the opinions are expressed by only one of the speakers, or whether the speakers agree. Write K for Kathy, D for Derek, or B for both, where they agree.*

You now have thirty seconds in which to look at Part Four.

[pause]

tone

Derek:	Have you seen that new film of *Oliver Twist*, Kathy?
Kathy:	Yes, I went last night. How about you?
Derek:	Saw it Monday. Good, isn't it?
Kathy:	Mm, it made me want to read the novel again.
Derek:	Me too, but there were so many actors I knew, I couldn't forget who they really were.
Kathy:	I know what you mean, but I can't say that worried me. I thought it was great seeing all those famous people.

Derek:	Still, it really brought the world of the novel to life.
Kathy:	Yes, there are so many films based on novels which end up falling between two stools, neither a good version of the novel nor something original.
Derek:	You know, it's interesting how, if you look at some 1930s and 40s films of 19th-century novels, they're really rooted in the period they were made, in the way people behaved and related to each other then.
Kathy:	Mm, I suppose so.
Derek:	And in the last few years, there's much more effort made to be authentic. Like how people walk. 19th-century clothes are so different from modern ones that people had to walk differently, and women were expected to take small steps. But in some old films the actors moved around as though they were wearing their own clothes. At least that doesn't happen so much these days.
Kathy:	But maybe if we saw today's films again in 20 years' time, they'd seem just as dated. It's because we're so close to them that we can't see that they're just as much reflections of *our* own time as the 30s films were of theirs. Maybe they actually show more about *us* and our values than about the novel that they're based on.
Derek:	Oh, surely directors and actors now are aware of the danger, so they actually *try* to get inside the minds of 19th-century people.
Kathy:	Well, we'll see. But you know what disturbs me sometimes is when I know the novel and have a clear picture of a character, and the actor is just wrong for the part.
Derek:	Like when the hero's supposed to be good-looking and you can't imagine anyone falling for him.
Kathy:	There was one film I had to walk out of, because the heroine was played as neurotic, and there wasn't a *hint* of that in the book.
Derek:	Mm. That sort of thing's taking artistic licence too far – if you're going to adapt a novel, you shouldn't make any major changes to the characters or the plot.
Kathy:	Actually, another thing that struck me is that in films I usually miss the author's voice.
Derek:	But he's sometimes there as an unseen narrator.
Kathy:	Mm, but in the novels the writer's there all the time, in little comments, and in films they either don't appear at all, or hardly.
Derek:	Do we need him at all? People make up their *own* minds about the characters. They don't need to be nudged in a particular direction by the author.
Kathy:	Do you think that's really possible? After all, the author's created the character and what they do, so we're manipulated into reacting to them in the way he wants us to.
Derek:	Look – suppose he approves of corporal punishment, say, and you don't. You'd judge a father beating his son differently from the way the author would.
Kathy:	Mm, but maybe it doesn't matter. Because usually we watch these films as escapism, don't we? Not as something to take too seriously.

[pause]

Now you'll hear Part Four again.

tone

[The recording is repeated.]

[pause]

That's the end of Part Four.

There'll now be a pause of five minutes for you to copy your answers onto the separate answer sheet. Be sure to follow the numbering of all the questions. I'll remind you when there is one minute left, so that you're sure to finish in time.

[pause]

You have one more minute left.

[pause]

That's the end of the test. Please stop now.

Test 3 Key

Paper 1   Reading (1 hour 30 minutes)

Part 1   (one mark for each correct answer)

1 B   2 B   3 D   4 D   5 C   6 A   7 B   8 A   9 C
10 D   11 A   12 B   13 B   14 C   15 B   16 A
17 D   18 D

Part 2   (two marks for each correct answer)

19 B   20 D   21 C   22 B   23 D   24 B   25 B   26 C

Part 3   (two marks for each correct answer)

27 C   28 H   29 D   30 G   31 F   32 A   33 E

Part 4   (two marks for each correct answer)

34 C   35 D   36 C   37 A   38 B   39 D   40 B

Paper 2   Writing (2 hours)

Task-specific mark schemes

Question 1

Content
Major points:
Discussion of:
- whether or not popular culture places emphasis on the importance of image and appearance
- whether or not this is producing a generation of people who are superficial, self-centred and materialistic.

Further points:
Relevant examples to agree or disagree with the statement.

Range
Language for expressing and supporting opinions, and for expressing disagreement.

Appropriacy of register and format
Formal letter format. Register appropriate to the writer's role as reader of a newspaper writing in to express opinions.

Organisation and cohesion
Clear organisation of points. Adequate use of paragraphing and linking.

Target reader
Would understand the writer's viewpoint.

136

Question 2

Content
The review should inform the readers about the book, explain the impact the work had on them as reader (element of personal anecdote is acceptable) and comment on its appeal for children.

Range
Language of description, analysis and evaluation.

Appropriacy of register and format
Register and format appropriate for a review in the Arts Section of a daily newspaper. Register can be formal/informal, but must be consistent.

Organisation and cohesion
Clear development of ideas. Adequate use of linking and paragraphing.

Target reader
Would be informed about the book and its appeal.
Would be able to decide whether to obtain it for themselves, for their own children or for children they know.

Question 3

Content
Description of the way of life in the past, with reference to relevant areas such as housing, clothes, food, customs, attitudes, etc.
Reasons for wanting to live at this period of time in the past.

Range
Language of description, analysis and explanation.

Appropriacy of register and format
Register and format appropriate for a magazine article, with possible use of section headings.

Organisation and cohesion
Clearly organised. Adequate use of linking and paragraphing.

Target reader
Would understand something about the period in history and why it was chosen.

Question 4

Content
Description of sporting and social events, details of future events, and an invitation to future members.

Range
Language of description, giving information and persuasion.

Appropriacy of register and format
Neutral/informal register that is friendly and encouraging in tone. Format appropriate to that of a report, possibly including section headings.

Organisation and cohesion
Clearly organised presentation of information. Appropriate paragraphing and linking.

Target reader
Would be well informed about past events, and would be interested in finding out more about the club and possibly joining.

Question 5(a)

Content
Clear reference to the book chosen.
Description and analysis of Macon's relationship with Muriel, and the reasons why he returns to her.

Range
Language of description, narrative and analysis.

Appropriacy of register and format
Neutral composition.

Organisation and cohesion
Clear presentation and development of ideas. Appropriate paragraphing and linking. Clear conclusion.

Target reader
Would understand Muriel's appeal for Macon, and why he returns to her.

Question 5(b)

Content
Clear reference to the book chosen.
Description of difficulties facing Josella and Bill, and an evaluation of whether the ending is happy or not.

Range
Language of description, narration and evaluation.

Appropriacy of register and format
Review with register and format appropriate for a magazine. Register must be consistent throughout.

Organisation and cohesion
Clear development from introduction to development of the main focus, leading to a clear conclusion.

Target reader
Would be informed about the difficulties facing Josella and Bill, the ending of the book and the writer's viewpoint.

Question 5(c)

Content
Clear reference to the book chosen.
Description of the portrayal of Hawthorne and the Chief.
Evaluation of their characters and whether or not they should be taken seriously.

Range
Language of description, narration, analysis and evaluation.

Appropriacy of register and format
Consistent and appropriate style for that of a report with possible use of headings.

Organisation and cohesion
Clear presentation and development of ideas, with appropriate linking and
paragraphing. The two parts of the question, description and evaluation, can be
dealt with separately or together. Clear conclusion.

Target reader
Would have a clear understanding of the writer's viewpoint with regard to whether
or not Hawthorne and the Chief should be portrayed in a serious or humorous
light.

Paper 3 Use of English (1 hour 30 minutes)

Part 1 (one mark for each correct answer)
1 into   2 may/might/can   3 terms   4 Regardless/regardless /
Irrespective/irrespective   5 time   6 at   7 for   8 Being/being
9 so   10 rather   11 result/consequence   12 let   13 What/what
14 this/that   15 however

Part 2 (one mark for each correct answer)
16 disposable   17 indifferent   18 attachment   19 cylindrical
20 intensity   21 basically   22 assertion   23 undoubted
24 exceptional   25 distinctive

Part 3 (two marks for each correct answer)
26 account   27 hold   28 face   29 rough   30 meet
31 wonder

Part 4 (one mark for each correct section)
32 I hadn't been (1) + taken in (1)
33 discussion (of the matter) was (1) + out of the (1)
34 for the ingenuity (1) + of his brother's (1)
35 with a view (1) + to opening (1)
36 was a sharp/marked/great contrast (1) + between (1)
37 a (very) slim / almost no / little chance (1) + of being given / of getting (1)
38 have a/any clue (1) + (about) how to (1)
39 did George make (1) + a complete recovery from (1)

Part 5   (questions 40–43 two marks for each correct answer)

40 (Employee's) oversights / slips and lapses / mistakes / employees who blunder / errors (any 2)

41 Searching for something or someone to blame for one's mistakes.

42 They expected a conventional meeting / to be instructed but were required to use artistic talent / to produce something / they did not expect to be making masks.

43 She thinks it is relatively uninteresting/unattractive in relation to other professions.

44 (one mark for each content point, up to ten marks for summary skills)
The paragraph should include the following points:
  i don't punish those who make mistakes
  ii reward those who cope with error
  iii have systems which can tolerate error
  iv encourage creativity / a sense of humour / self-expression

Paper 4   Listening (40 minutes approximately)

Part 1   (one mark for each correct answer)

1 B   2 A   3 B   4 C   5 A   6 B   7 C   8 B

Part 2   (one mark for each correct answer)

9 sandy   10 dozen   11 notice(-)boards   12 pruning   13 cereal(s)
14 roots   15 roof(-)tiles / making roofs/roof(-)tiles   16 desert
17 Spanish eagle(s)

Part 3   (one mark for each correct answer)

18 B   19 C   20 A   21 B   22 C

Part 4   (one mark for each correct answer)

23 L   24 S   25 B   26 L   27 B   28 S

Transcript   *Certificate of Proficiency in English Listening Test. Test 3.*

I'm going to give you the instructions for this test.

I'll introduce each part of the test and give you time to look at the questions.

At the start of each piece you'll hear this sound:

tone

You'll hear each piece twice.

Remember, while you're listening, write your answers on the question paper.

You'll have five minutes at the end of the test to copy your answers onto the separate answer sheet.

There will now be a pause. Please ask any questions now, because you must not speak during the test.

[pause]

Now open your question paper and look at Part One.

[pause]

PART 1

You'll hear four different extracts. For questions 1 to 8, choose the answer (A, B or C) which fits best according to what you hear. There are two questions for each extract.

Extract 1

[pause]

tone

Interviewer:	So, how do you get the fish in the first place? Do you buy them or breed them here?
Margot:	No, I don't rely on anyone else, I'm thankfully self-sufficient in juveniles, the young ones, because I breed my own fish here as this enables me to give full details of the fishes' origins to customers. They expect that.
Interviewer:	Which part of the whole process do you enjoy most?
Margot:	Really, product development is my baby, and one has to put one's mind to that continuously. It's crucial.
Interviewer:	The marketing skill that you've developed here with your fish – would that be transferable to beef, sheep …?
Margot:	Well, I think it's a mindset, isn't it? To my mind, producing fish is fantastic, it's a great satisfaction to do it properly, but you know, what's the point of producing a wonderful fish if you haven't got a profitable sale at the end of the day? I think it comes down to providing a top quality service for your clients. And I must say, that's really what I enjoy. That's what keeps me here.

[pause]

tone

[The recording is repeated.]

[pause]

Extract 2

[pause]

tone

Interviewer:	So, did you feel, when you started publishing, that women were treated differently from men, by critics, for example?

Novelist: It never crossed my mind, so confident was I that I could do it. I think if you start counting the low numbers of reviews and contributors to literary journals, you do get a rather dismal answer. But that didn't worry me. And I think one of the reasons was that writing novels is, for a woman, the best choice to make. There was a long tradition behind you. Had I chosen other forms of literary endeavour like drama, which I did have a go at and failed, it would have been very different. There was a huge gap in England between Aphra Behn, the infamous woman playwright of the sixteenth century, and the next really successful woman dramatist, Caryl Churchill, in the 1960s! I was very conscious in drama of not exactly an establishment, but all sorts of things I couldn't cope with or got frustrated by. The novel was uniquely the sphere in which you felt you had equal billing.

[pause]

tone

[The recording is repeated.]

[pause]

Extract 3   [pause]

tone

Presenter: I haven't read the Inspector Rebus books myself. What's he like?
Actor: Well, he's kind of concerned about his place within the world. He's quite …
Presenter: He's a thinker.
Actor: Yeah, in the way that we all are. We think, what on earth's going on? How can this happen? Am I part of the problem, or in some way part of the solution? What am I doing to change that? And in a very sort of introspective way I think he tries to resolve his own life issues by dealing with them externally.
Presenter: He's a bit of an independent thinker, an eccentric, then?
Actor: Well, yes. But that's probably because, as an individual, he's concerned with what is happening to him and to the world, and I think being a cop is often, in some sense, a kind of, a kind of pursuit, theoretical or psychological, trying to understand the world that he lives in, through trying to understand the events that happen around him. So he's anti the authorities in general, certainly, but I think he's probably just more aware of his personal responsibility for his own existence than – than simply eccentric.

[pause]

tone

[The recording is repeated.]

[pause]

Extract 4   [pause]

tone

Speaker: What's strange about pop music is that it usually has a clear function. The function of the music of the 1940s and 50s was to soothe and to bring romance back into life. In the sixties the function was simply to help young people to make the transition from adolescence to adulthood. That was all it was about. It provided a self-contained therapy, which had never been necessary before. This rite of passage had always been eased by society, by the military system, by the academic, by the post industrial revolution machinery. By the end of the fifties the young had shaken themselves free of all that, they had to look after themselves and the popular culture reflected that. We forget that before the 1960s young people generally aspired to be like their parents in styles of dress, work, even leisure. Then, suddenly the rebellious independent teenager was born. It was a totally new concept, which initially shook the older generation to the core as youth took over and revolutionised fashion, lifestyle, travel and, of course, morals.

[pause]

tone

[The recording is repeated.]

[pause]

That's the end of Part One.

Now turn to Part Two.

[pause]

PART 2 *You'll hear a lecture on the cork forests of southern Spain and Portugal. For questions 9 to 17, complete the sentences with a word or short phrase.*

You now have forty-five seconds in which to look at Part Two.

[pause]

tone

Presenter: Good morning. Today's lecture is about the humble cork. And here to tell us about it is cork farmer, Roger Reynard.

Roger: Thank you. Well let's start by establishing what cork is exactly. We all know it as the light spongy substance used for covering food and drink in bottles and jars. Fewer people know that it comes from the bark of a pretty little oak tree which, surprisingly, requires sandy soil to thrive. I have been farming cork in the more barren areas of southern Spain and Portugal for 20 years and am proud of the fact that our area produces 85% of the world's supply *and* also contributes to the maintenance of an ancient agricultural eco-system.

Let's have a look at a picture of a typical cork forest. As you can see, the trees have a distinct, crusty bark. Every nine years, during the months of May, June, July and August, the outer layer is stripped off. Cork can be collected from a tree as many as a dozen times in its productive life. In its processing, the cork is firstly seasoned in giant stacks and then, after that, it's boiled for an hour or more. It is then graded for its quality: a top quality cork will fetch ten times more than a cheaper grade which is harder and has more knobs on it, so it would be used not for jar and bottle stoppers but for shoe soles, roof tiling and, principally, noticeboards – these don't have to have the flexibility and smoothness we expect in an expensive cork. So it's a resource which has many uses, though, of course, it is best known as a cover or stopper on food and drink containers. It's this use which gets the best returns for us farmers and enables the cork forests to be maintained. Quality therefore has to be every cork farmer's aim and this is sustained by correct levels of fertilisation, but *most* importantly, suitable pruning, because this allows the trees to spread and therefore flourish.

As I indicated earlier, these forests have been growing for as long as 2,000 years and this ancient environment has developed a thriving eco-system with healthy bio-diversity. As you can see from the picture, cereals are sown between the rows of trees, helping to maintain the soils. Going back to the tree, of course, you do not only reap the cork *bark*; acorns from the tree are also valuable in these traditional agricultural systems, used for feed for animals such as sheep, which graze on the adjacent scrub-land.

This system is the product of a web which has been slowly spun over many years. What might bring it to an end is something called TCA, or to give it its full name two-four-six-trichloranysol. Tiny traces of this occasionally cause foods and drink to taste musty. No one knows for sure how it gets into cork and this is why a solution to the problem is such a long time coming. I have a theory about it though: that it comes from the roots of different species of trees growing near the cork oaks. I'm pleased to say I have managed to persuade the local Cork Growers Association to cut the affected section of all trees grown in our area and send it for use in roof tiles, where the toxicity is not problematic.

I suggest that these measures should be instituted in all cork growing areas very soon because, although some people are aware of the threat, others feel that, with TCA, plastic will replace cork entirely. But this decline of the cork industry in the south of Spain and Portugal will then lead to the loss of cork forests and turn the land into a desert. Not only will it wipe out an ancient crop but also the environment which supports a myriad of unique species, most notably the Spanish eagle. Cork is one of the few products which maintains the delicate ecological balance of this fragile environment and many people feel its survival is worth fighting for.

[pause]

Now you'll hear Part Two again.

tone

[The recording is repeated.]

[pause]

That's the end of Part Two.

Now turn to Part Three.

[pause]

PART 3   *You'll hear part of a radio programme about a group of people on an expedition to the South Pole. For questions 18 to 22, choose the answer (A, B, C or D) which fits best according to what you hear.*

You now have one minute in which to look at Part Three.

[pause]

tone

Interviewer: I caught up with the all-woman team as they rested in their tent about 350 kilometres away from the South Pole. The expedition started in November. They walk about 40 kilometres a day pulling sledges laden with their supplies and equipment. I asked Caroline, the team leader, to describe what life was like.

Caroline: Well, the sun is shining, there's a beautiful blue sky, but it's very cold. It's about minus 25 degrees Centigrade. We've got stacks of underwear and a large sort of poncho and dungarees which keep us very warm; hat, hood and then a face mask as well, which is vital to keep the wind out. There are five of us together and we go along in single file so there isn't much chance of a conversation.

Interviewer: Isn't it a very lonely experience?

Caroline: Well, it gives us time to daydream and it's also incredibly beautiful, so there's lots to look at and we do need to concentrate very hard, one foot in front of the other in order to keep momentum going. We've all got big heavy sledges behind us and so the sledges pull on you and they get caught in ridges and things, and so you've got to keep fighting against your sledge to make sure you keep moving along.

Interviewer: Two years ago when you organised the first female expedition to the North Pole, obviously that was an arduous task that you had. How does it compare with this one?

Caroline: It's obviously harder because we're going the whole distance. Last time it was a relay and I was on the last leg of the relay, for instance, and did 160 kilometres. This time it's over a thousand.

Interviewer: Now during the last expedition, I think it was Pom Oliver who did fall through the ice and dislocate her shoulder, have you had any hairy moments this time?

Caroline: Well crevasses, we've come up against, you know, incredibly deep cracks in the ice, we've had to negotiate our way around them. The first time we had that, it was a bit hairy, especially in a white-out of snow when you can't see anything; then there was an occasion a couple of days ago when we heard rumblings coming up from beneath the ice, and a lot of banging and crashing below which was, I found very unnerving.

Interviewer: I know that you're working a lot because of travelling so far every day and obviously you're pitching your tent every day. How is the practical work of getting your tent up for the night done?

Caroline: We all put up the tent together and we've got a routine where we all know which pole we put in. We put the inner tent in. Then Pom goes in because we've made a 3 millimetre floor on the bottom of the tent to keep it warm and obviously to keep our feet warm. So we all work together as a team to get it up but the cooker's on as quick as we can. And as soon as everyone's in hopefully by then the hot water's boiling and we can have hot soup and cheese – without that I'd be dead on my feet.

Interviewer:	And do you always sleep well?
Caroline:	As soon as our heads touch the sleeping bags we're out cold. We always get our full eight hours' sleep and the next thing you know the alarm is going off.
Interviewer:	Now, Caroline, earlier this week, I'm sure you're aware of this, another team reached the South Pole before you. Has this been demoralising for you and your team?
Caroline:	No, not at all. It's just one of those things. I'm really thrilled that they've got there. We know them and their guide a bit, and we've spoken to them a few times on the journey, so we knew that they were nearly there. We've done the North Pole. We want to do the South Pole. We're all women, the first all women British expedition. The other expedition was not at all the same in its nature; it was a mixed group, commercially organised. So no hard feelings at all.

[pause]

Now you'll hear Part Three again.

tone

[The recording is repeated.]

[pause]

That's the end of Part Three.

Now turn to Part Four.

[pause]

PART 4   *You'll hear part of a radio programme in which two people, Louise and Stephen, discuss a film they have recently seen. For questions 23 to 28, decide whether the opinions are expressed by only one of the speakers, or whether the speakers agree. Write L for Louise, S for Stephen, or B for both, where they agree.*

You now have thirty seconds in which to look at Part Four.

[pause]

tone

Louise:	Well, Stephen, the new film directed by John Bernard, *Life in America*, I think the thing that really amazes me about this film is that it got made by a major studio at all, because the film pokes fun at almost everything that corporate and suburban America hold dear – you know, a nice life, material wealth, self-help philosophy. It really sends up almost everything you can think of and it does it very well!
Stephen:	I was less enraptured, Louise. To me it seemed too well-trodden a path to involve much irony and, let's face it, it was extraordinarily pedestrian. Visually as well, although there were some very lovely moments, it seemed rather trite, which I was amazed by.
Louise:	Hmm, do you mean like when we kept on seeing those young girls covered in rose petals from the garden … pedestrian is going too far, though. The treatment seemed to be that of a young director enamoured like a kid with the process of film making, and I don't think that's a bad thing. I think he's got a great enthusiasm and passion and probably a great film career ahead of him.

Stephen: Well, that goes without saying. But I think if you go to this film with huge expectations, you can only be disappointed. But at the same time there's so much that's humorous, there are a number of new and subtle twists on perennial themes.

Louise: The core of the subject matter is certainly familiar, but this film does look at some aspects from a different angle. I mean I particularly liked the way the father/daughter relationship developed. And I really think it does have its sublime moments.

Stephen: Do you? I tell you what I think is really interesting and subversive about this film. At one point it looks as if you're going to have a happy ending involving serious crime, and I couldn't believe that a mainstream American movie was going to suggest that crime was a good way to get out of your problems.

Louise: It almost does as a matter of fact. And, come to think of it, we don't get the usual reassuring moral message reinforced in the final moments as we're left sort of suspended.

Stephen: Hmm, it's an interesting idea. Everybody comes out of the cinema trying to work out how it will all wind up. But what's so wonderful about *this* film is the camera work. Young directors often use the power and energy of the camera to get a kinetic sense of excitement. This film is amazingly processional and calm and you get these wonderful slow movements which open up your heart at times.

Louise: Mmm, I see what you mean, though a little more tension might have enhanced the balance of the whole, although it would have to be judiciously added ...

[pause]

Now you'll hear Part Four again.

tone

[The recording is repeated.]

[pause]

That's the end of Part Four.

There'll now be a pause of five minutes for you to copy your answers onto the separate answer sheet. Be sure to follow the numbering of all the questions. I'll remind you when there is one minute left, so that you're sure to finish in time.

[pause]

You have one more minute left.

[pause]

That's the end of the test. Please stop now.

Test 4 Key

Paper 1   Reading (1 hour 30 minutes)

Part 1   (one mark for each correct answer)
1 C   2 B   3 B   4 C   5 A   6 D   7 C   8 D   9 A
10 C   11 A   12 B   13 D   14 A   15 C   16 C
17 B   18 D

Part 2   (two marks for each correct answer)
19 B   20 D   21 C   22 A   23 C   24 A   25 A   26 D

Part 3   (two marks for each correct answer)
27 E   28 F   29 H   30 G   31 A   32 D   33 C

Part 4   (two marks for each correct answer)
34 C   35 B   36 C   37 A   38 D   39 D   40 D

Paper 2   Writing (2 hours)

Task-specific mark schemes

Question 1
Content
Major points:
The following points will need addressing:
- books in competition with TV and computers, and perhaps becoming less popular
- books providing a unique pleasure
- books as convenient and just as rewarding as TV or computers.

Further points:
Popularity of video rather than books.
Other reasons why people read books.

Range
Language for expressing and supporting opinions, and for defending or attacking an argument, depending on individual viewpoint.

Appropriacy of register and format
Register appropriate to the writer's role as reader of a newspaper submitting an article for a media magazine. Article may make use of headings.

Organisation and cohesion
Clear development of argument. Adequate use of linking and paragraphing.

148

Target reader
Would understand the writer's viewpoint.

Question 2

Content
Range of reasons for wanting to take part.
Speculation about what they would hope to learn from the experience.

Range
Language of description (e.g. personal qualities), persuasion and speculation.

Appropriacy of register and format
Formal or neutral register (though must be consistent) and format appropriate for a letter to a television company.

Organisation and cohesion
Clear organisation and development of ideas with appropriate linking and paragraphing.

Target reader
TV producers would be interested in having this person in the programme.

Question 3

Content
Relative merits of dinner, disco, concert and other ideas.
Recommendation of the best idea.

Range
Language of recommendation and persuasive argument.

Appropriacy of register and format
Register and format appropriate for a proposal with possible use of headings.
Register can be neutral/informal, but must be consistent.

Organisation and cohesion
Clearly organised treatment of each suggestion and other ideas. Final recommendation must be clearly expressed decision.

Target reader
Would know exactly what was recommended and why.

Question 4

Content
Description of scenes/narrative elements of films.
Explanation of what makes the film funny / different types of humour.
Reasons for recommending the film for the award.

Range
Language of description, narration, contrast and recommendation.

Appropriacy of register and format
Register and format appropriate for a review in a film magazine.

Organisation and cohesion
Clear development of narrative detail and description. Appropriate paragraphing and linking. Clear conclusion.

Target reader
Would be interested in seeing the film and understand why it is funny and successful.

Question 5(a)

Content
Clear reference to the book chosen.
Description and analysis of the character and importance of the dog, Edward.
Evaluation of the statement and whether or not it is true for this novel.

Range
Language of description, narration and evaluation.

Appropriacy of register and format
Formal letter.

Organisation and cohesion
Clear presentation and development of ideas with appropriate linking of paragraphs from the introduction to the main body of the letter and the conclusion.

Target reader
Would understand the writer's viewpoint with regard to whether a dog can have a significant role in a novel for adults.

Question 5(b)

Content
Clear reference to the book chosen.
Comparison of Tynsham and Shirning, with a description of the people and the way they live their lives there.
Evaluation of the effect these places and people have on Bill Masen.

Range
Language of description, narration, comparison and evaluation.

Appropriacy of register and format
Neutral composition.

Organisation and cohesion
Clear presentation and development of ideas. Appropriate paragraphing and linking. Clear conclusion.

Target reader
Would have a clear idea of what both places were like, how the occupants felt about living there, and how they affect Bill Masen.

Question 5(c)

Content
Close reference to the book chosen.
Description and comparison of Hawthorne's views on service to one's country, and Wormold's views on loyalty to one's friends.

Range
Language of description, narration, comparison and evaluation.

Appropriacy of register and format
Neutral composition.

Organisation and cohesion
Clear presentation and development of ideas. Appropriate paragraphing and linking. Clear conclusion.

Target reader
Would have a clear idea of the attitudes of both characters.

Paper 3   Use of English (1 hour 30 minutes)

Part 1   (one mark for each correct answer)

1 It/it   2 to   3 sooner   4 order   5 Should/should   6 run/face
7 come   8 Given/given   9 without   10 a   11 will
12 this/it/she   13 anything/anyone/anybody   14 if NOT when
15 despite/in

Part 2   (one mark for each correct answer)

16 necessarily   17 reluctance   18 characteristic   19 likelihood
20 presumably   21 significance   22 insecurity   23 appreciative
24 unaware   25 loneliness

Part 3   (two marks for each correct answer)

26 turn   27 steps   28 picture   29 admission   30 faint
31 capital

Part 4   (one mark for each correct section)

32 to (a/the) popular belief (1) + not all (1)
33 shyness was due to (1) + (a/his) lack (1)
34 believe his luck (1) + when he (NOT had) (1)
35 nowhere (1) + until / but then / then John came up with (1)
36 lacks awareness (1) + when it (1)
37 take the clock apart (1) + unless (1)
38 broken thumb / injury to his thumb / thumb injury (1) + affect his ability (1)
39 she had not / hadn't (1) + turned down (1)

Part 5   (questions 40–43 two marks for each correct answer)

40 spontaneity may be eliminated / performers may not perform well / music may no longer be 'great'
41 any paraphrase of 'peculiar temperament' / a solitary/strange personality
42 He is not distracted by what is happening around him.
43 minor flaws
44 (up to four marks for content points, up to ten marks for summary skills)
   The paragraph should include the following points:
   i More than one interpretation of music is possible.
   ii more spontaneity/emotion at a live concert
   iii You get a feel for the personality of the performers.
   iv the interaction the performers have with the audience and vice versa
   v You can be oblivious to imperfections.

Paper 4   Listening (40 minutes approximately)

Part 1   (one mark for each correct answer)
1 A   **2** C   **3** B   **4** C   **5** A   **6** B   **7** C   **8** B

Part 2   (one mark for each correct answer)
9 misconception/misapprehension (NOT belief/conviction/mistake)
10 (pressure) wave   **11** brain   **12** location/position
13 hunter (for food)   **14** (if there is) (any) distress (NOT crying)
15 (the moment of) birth   **16** washing machine (sound/noise)
17 letters of complaint / complaints / reports

Part 3   (one mark for each correct answer)
18 B   **19** C   **20** A   **21** D   **22** B

Part 4   (one mark for each correct answer)
23 S   **24** S   **25** B   **26** S   **27** T   **28** T

Transcript   *Certificate of Proficiency in English Listening Test. Test 4.*

I'm going to give you the instructions for this test.

I'll introduce each part of the test and give you time to look at the questions.

At the start of each piece you'll hear this sound:

tone

You'll hear each piece twice.

Remember, while you're listening, write your answers on the question paper.

> *You'll have five minutes at the end of the test to copy your answers onto the separate answer sheet.*
>
> *There will now be a pause. Please ask any questions now, because you must not speak during the test.*
>
> [pause]
>
> *Now open your question paper and look at Part One.*
>
> [pause]

PART 1 *You'll hear four different extracts. For questions 1 to 8, choose the answer (A, B or C) which fits best according to what you hear. There are two questions for each extract.*

Extract 1 [pause]

tone

Speaker: Is wordplay at the heart of the English language? Before I started looking at this I would have laughed to scorn the idea that wordplay was anything more than a playground activity that children delight in or part of a comedian's patter. The more I go into it the more I find. It is in fact an integral part of the way the language works and forms much of what constitutes communication.

  And I am reminded of the 19th century writer George Eliot who said 'a different taste in jokes places a great strain on the affections'. And there is a great truth here – that people who really bond well together enjoy each other's wordplay, whatever it is, whether it's a pun or a joke. And when the day comes that somebody in a relationship says 'Why are you always making those stupid jokes?', we know it won't last much longer. So wordplay, it seems to me, can be an immensely serious business at times.

[pause]

tone

[The recording is repeated.]

[pause]

Extract 2 [pause]

tone

Speaker: Many actors say that doing the voices for animated films is the hardest acting job they have ever done, because when they come into the recording studio there's nothing around them: no costumes, no actors, no special lighting, and yet they do a remarkable job. As director, I go in and describe to them the set, the other characters, what kind of noises there are going to be, and I try to paint a picture in their minds and then I let them go.

We video tape each of our recording sessions for the animators because what the actors do in front of a microphone with their facial expressions and their hand gestures is so remarkable that the animators get inspired by it. They don't copy it directly, but they get inspired by it to the point where each of the actors that does the voice for one of our characters, when they see the final movie, they'll say, 'That's me, I never knew I was like a toy cowboy', but it is them, because there is so much of them in the gestures and the expressions.

[pause]

tone

[The recording is repeated.]

[pause]

Extract 3   [pause]

tone

Interviewer: As an eminent environmentalist, you have devoted your life to this subject and I haven't, but nevertheless I have tried to find some evidence which contradicts your views; because I'm worried about how you can know so much about what's going to happen in a hundred years' time, and I'm worried about the way you support your argument. You say things have come and gone, repeated themselves over the last few thousand years, but your statistics only go back a hundred years, so what are you measuring it against? That worries me. I came across this article by Peter Dennis and he agrees with much of what you say, but between 900 and 1300 AD, the earth's temperature rose by 4 to 7 degrees Fahrenheit, very close to your predictions of this 21st century. It was one of the most favourable periods in human history. The population actually boomed, food production expanded, there was a surplus of workers and energy, colossal buildings were required and built, minerals were mined, the deserts retreated, etc., etc. So in those years he has evidence that things got massively better for people …

[pause]

tone

[The recording is repeated.]

[pause]

Extract 4   [pause]

tone

Presenter: So, Pauline, were you laughed at in the playground when you were playing football?
Interviewee: Not at all, actually. The best player in my primary school was a girl. So no problems with that.
Presenter: And how many girls at university played football?
Interviewer: Well, at university we just had the one women's team. It was very informal, it was just a social thing. If you wanted to play seriously, you had to go off and find a league to join.

Presenter:	How do you think more women could be encouraged to join the game?
Interviewee:	We must show people good strong role models. This myth about women not being able to play football, we need to get rid of that. We need to say yes, we can succeed in the game. And also the families need to see that it's a career their child can take. For a boy who wants to make it at the top level, that's a career choice, and I suppose parents think of football as a hobby for a girl, not a career. If they see it's an option for them, it'll work.

[pause]

tone

[The recording is repeated.]

[pause]

That's the end of Part One.

Now turn to Part Two.

[pause]

PART 2   *You'll hear part of a radio programme about the sense of hearing. For questions 9 to 17, complete the sentences with a word or short phrase.*

You now have forty-five seconds in which to look at Part Two.

[pause]

tone

Speaker:	Today I'm going to look at the sense of hearing, one of those senses that can fade with age. In general, provided that we don't know of a problem with our hearing, we tend to assume that we all hear the same thing. But, in fact, this seems to be a misconception because men and women are increasingly claiming that there are disparities in what they hear. So are they right? Do men and women have different auditory experiences? Here's how it all works. Sound meets the outer ear, which has the form of a funnel. The sound passes through this to the eardrum. Then three tiny bones send what is known as a pressure wave down to the inner ear where the sound message is encoded. Finally, in a fraction of a second, the information passes up through the auditory nerve to the brain and we realise that we've heard a sound.
	The most fascinating thing about the inside of the ear is that a part that measures three millimetres in a child of ten will also measure three millimetres in a very tall adult. But can men and women's hearing vary despite this uniformity? An Australian biologist Alan Treece is adamant that they can. He believes that men are better at discerning the location of a sound than women. Thus, he suggests that if you wake a man up and there's a dog howling in the distance, most men can generally point to where the sound is coming from. The original purpose would seem to be that in prehistoric times, man, as the hunter, had to chase wild animals for food. It therefore made sense that he could hear sounds in the distance and was able to identify where they originated from so that he could catch his prey. Treece is also convinced that women are genetically programmed

to hear crying babies, a handy excuse perhaps for all those men who would rather stay in bed than attend to a screaming infant! Treece puts it down to the fact that women hear better than men in terms of distinguishing high-pitched sounds. He links this to the fact that women as the child bearers need the ability to hear if there is any distress coming from the child. But it does seem that when the role of carer is reversed, men are mysteriously equally good at hearing their offspring.

So what's the scientific truth behind such ideas? Do men and women really differ in their hearing? An ongoing study at Cambridge University shows that some differences have been found. By putting a tiny microphone inside the ear it has been possible to measure that women's hearing is slightly better than men's. And this difference is observable from the moment of birth. Other studies have shown that the right ear tends to be better than the left.

One mysterious difference between the sexes was highlighted recently when a number of women in Manchester started hearing strange sounds, which their husbands simply couldn't. The sound is a low continuous noise similar to that which a washing machine makes. It is less noticeable at some times than it is at others. For some reason it seems to be very loud at the weekends, during the night. The sufferers hear this noise when they go to bed and it prevents them from going to sleep. Some say that the sound seems to be piercing their heads. The local council has failed to work out what the sounds can be. What is really intriguing is that all the complaints sent in to the Council offices so far have been from women. No man seems to be able to hear it. So I hope that this has given you a preliminary insight into the mysterious world of sound. I will look at some further research projects in this area in my next talk ...

[pause]

Now you'll hear Part Two again.

tone

[The recording is repeated.]

[pause]

That's the end of Part Two.

Now turn to Part Three.

[pause]

PART 3   *You'll hear a book reviewer on a radio programme about science discussing a book about the human brain. For questions 18 to 22, choose the answer (A, B, C or D) which fits best according to what you hear.*

You now have one minute in which to look at Part Three.

[pause]

tone

Presenter: And now here's Peter Hughes with our regular book review feature. Peter, what have you been reading this week?

Peter:	It's a book called *Mapping the mind*, which is about research into the human brain.
Presenter:	Neuroscience?
Peter:	That's right. Until recently, we couldn't directly examine what was going on in the brain. But nowadays new imaging techniques make all this visible.
Presenter:	Like X-rays revealing our bones?
Peter:	Exactly. In this case mapping means locating the precise brain activity that creates particular experiences and behaviours. It's a fascinating subject, because neuroscience is revealing a great deal about our actions.
Presenter:	Let's have some examples of how brain activity affects our behaviour.
Peter:	Well, we can now identify how electrical activity in different parts of the brain causes feelings of anger, violence, kindness, self-awareness, and so on. For instance one area of the brain lights up when we register a joke, and a different area glows dully when we recall an unhappy memory.
Presenter:	Does this change our view of personality?
Peter:	It certainly does. We're finding out that the thoughts and emotions that make up our personalities reflect *biological* mechanisms, suggesting that our personalities are actually formed by what goes on in our brains.
Presenter:	Which sounds like a very important discovery.
Peter:	Yes, both practically and socially. For one thing, it paves the way for us to *control* brain activity quite precisely. Compare it with what we're learning about the body, about how the DNA sequences that we have in our genes can make one person fat, for instance, and another suffer from a certain illness. We're beginning to be able to do something to treat those conditions, through genetic engineering.
Presenter:	Can we modify both the brain and the body?
Peter:	Not just yet, but it won't be that long till they're both possible. Though according to the author, control of the brain is probably nearer, because unlike human genetic engineering, it doesn't depend on the development of tricky new technology. All it needs is a little refinement of existing methods and techniques, like drugs and surgery, which at the moment are rather hit-and-miss. But it won't be long before we can target treatments precisely enough to control an individual's state of mind – and that will affect their behaviour.
Presenter:	It's surprising how little we hear about the potential uses of neuroscientists' work, considering that it's such a new field and they're already at the leading edge of scientific research.
Peter:	And scientific findings are normally hyped, in the scramble for funding. Yes, it's partly because neuroscientists have come into the discipline from many different fields, and they're so busy charting brain functions that they haven't yet developed a group mentality or a consensus about their long-term purpose. And of course, many of them are terrified of the scrutiny and government control that might result from tabloid publicity, so they're happy to keep a low profile.
Presenter:	It's rather ironic, isn't it, that while we're all terribly concerned about genetic engineering, we hear so little about brain mapping.
Peter:	Yes, it tends to be regarded as 'interesting for those who like that sort of thing, but of no practical importance'.

Presenter:	And is that where this book comes in?
Peter:	Mmm. The author wants to open up the debate on the implications of this research, both for society and for our understanding of consciousness. She focuses on brain mapping, although, as she points out, this is only one part of the picture: there are also the extremely complex *interactions* of the brain's various parts, which she's only touched on. And I wish she'd given us at least an overview of discoveries in that area.
Presenter:	Finally, Peter, who is this book for?
Peter:	Well, it's an exploration of virgin territory, that deals with a complex subject clearly and without dumbing it down. People who prefer to travel only on well-worn paths should wait for the tourist guides that'll be along later. But those who enjoy exploring will discover some strange and wonderful things here.
Presenter:	Peter Hughes, thank you.
Peter:	Thank you.

[pause]

Now you'll hear Part Three again.

tone

[The recording is repeated.]

[pause]

That's the end of Part Three.

Now turn to Part Four.

[pause]

PART 4

You'll hear part of a radio programme in which two writers, Tanya and Sam, discuss writing. For questions 23 to 28, decide whether the opinions are expressed by only one of the speakers, or whether the speakers agree. Write T for Tanya, S for Sam, or B for both, where they agree.

You now have thirty seconds in which to look at Part Four.

[pause]

tone

Presenter:	Today we have two writers in the studio. Welcome, Tanya Tallis and Sam Whateley.
Tanya/Sam:	Hello.
Presenter:	Sam, it's sometimes said that writers as a group have more in common than they diverge. What's your opinion on this?
Sam:	One of the things I think you can safely say about writers is that our driving force is the itch for fame and recognition.
Tanya:	*I* think if *anything* we're a neurotic lot driven by our internal demons. I mean, every writer I know seems to be this lethal combination of sometimes coming on far too strong, and at others acting like a frightened rabbit. Though I wouldn't be surprised if both stem from the same demon of insecurity.

Sam: That's rather a generalisation, isn't it? I know what you mean about coming on too strong, and it *is* often to compensate for something. Though don't you need to be pretty sure of yourself to assert yourself on paper? After all, why should people want to read my thoughts on whatever?

Tanya: I'd call it a need to write, rather than a need to be read, and that hardly comes from being sure of yourself.

Sam: Well, another thing we have in common is our uncertainty about the business side of things. That's all we talk about when we get together.

Tanya: Mm, it's all grumbles about publishers, editors and so on. In fact I tend to avoid congregations of writers purely because you get so much whingeing, and often it just gets you more steamed up.

Sam: You *do* get plenty of that. I try to sift through it to find out which editors are supportive and which ones to avoid. And anyway, often it's very difficult for a writer to know how much to charge for a particular piece of work, and unless you talk to other writers, you can't find out the going rate.

Tanya: But don't you think what's maddening about the term 'writer' is that anyone can be one? You know, it's not like hairdressing. I mean, I don't think, if I'm short of a few quid, 'Oh, I'll go and cut a few people's hair, I'm sure I'll make a reasonable fist of it,' but any old superannuated celebrity or politician can pick up a pen and get away with it.

Sam: Don't you think though that people realise that, let's call it 'real literature', is in a different league from a celeb's ghosted tripe? They know there's an awful lot of craft involved in writing, and it takes years to learn it.

Tanya: But do we *want* literature to be, if you like, all craft and no inspiration? Surely inspiration is paramount.

Sam: Of course you need the germ of the idea that you want to develop in the first place, but I wouldn't underestimate the technique side of things. I can think of two or three novels based on very banal concepts that've been turned into something quite stunning.

Tanya: So have *you* got anything up your sleeve to '*stun*' us with?

Sam: Um ...

Tanya: Oh come on, we all know we *should* keep our cards close to our chests, but being writers we need to bounce our ideas off someone.

Sam: Well I've known so many people who've had their ideas ripped off. You know, they bob up in other people's work if you share them, and most of us have learnt from that now.

Presenter: There I'm afraid we must stop, because it's time for the news. Thank you both very much indeed.

Sam/Tanya: Thank you.

[pause]

Now you'll hear Part Four again.

tone

[The recording is repeated.]

[pause]

That's the end of Part Four.

There'll now be a pause of five minutes for you to copy your answers onto the separate answer sheet. Be sure to follow the numbering of all the questions. I'll remind you when there is one minute left, so that you're sure to finish in time.

[pause]

You have one more minute left.

[pause]

That's the end of the test. Please stop now.

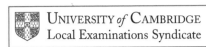

UNIVERSITY *of* CAMBRIDGE
Local Examinations Syndicate

 P LE

Candidate Name
If not already printed write name
in CAPITALS and complete the
Candidate No. grid (in pencil)

Candidate's signature

Examination Title

Centre

Supervisor:

if the candidate is ABSENT or has WITHDRAWN shade here ⬜

Centre No.

Candidate No.

Examination Details

0	0	0	0
1	1	1	1
2	2	2	2
3	3	3	3
4	4	4	4
5	5	5	5
6	6	6	6
7	7	7	7
8	8	8	8
9	9	9	9

Candidate Answer Sheet

Instructions
Use a soft PENCIL(B or HB).

Mark ONE letter only for each question.

For example, if you think **B** is the right answer, mark your answer sheet in pencil like this:

0   A   B   C   D

Rub out any answer you wish to change.

Part 1
1–18: A B C D

Part 2
19–26: A B C D

Part 4
34–40: A B C D

Part 3
27–33: A B C D E F G H

Sample answer sheet: Paper 3

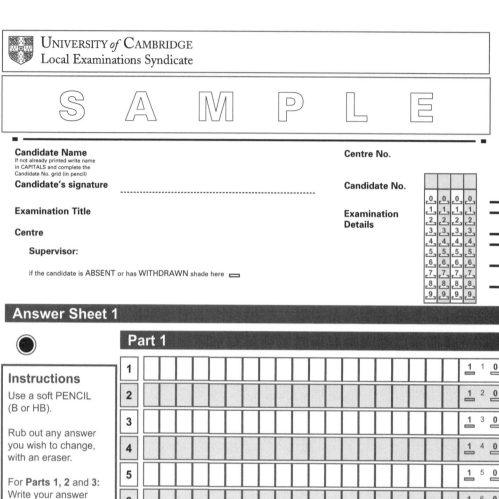

UNIVERSITY *of* CAMBRIDGE
Local Examinations Syndicate

S A M P L E

Candidate Name
If not already printed write name
in CAPITALS and complete the
Candidate No. grid (in pencil)

Candidate's signature

Examination Title

Centre

Supervisor:

if the candidate is ABSENT or has WITHDRAWN shade here

Centre No.

Candidate No.

Examination Details

Answer Sheet 1

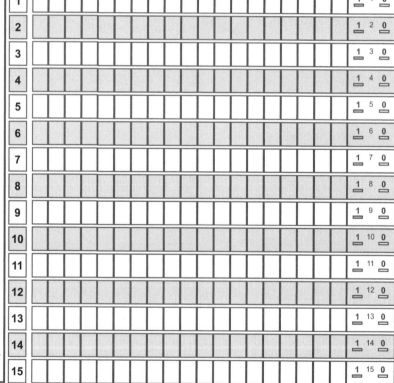

Part 1

Instructions

Use a soft PENCIL
(B or HB).

Rub out any answer
you wish to change,
with an eraser.

For **Parts 1, 2** and **3:**
Write your answer
clearly in CAPITAL
LETTERS.
Write one letter in each
box.

For example:

0 M A Y

Answer **Parts 4 and 5**
on the second answer
sheet.

Write your answer
neatly in the spaces
provided.

You do not have to
write in capital letters for
Parts 4 and 5.

162

Part 2

16		1 16 0
17		1 17 0
18		1 18 0
19		1 19 0
20		1 20 0
21		1 21 0
22		1 22 0
23		1 23 0
24		1 24 0
25		1 25 0

Part 3

26		1 26 0
27		1 27 0
28		1 28 0
29		1 29 0
30		1 30 0
31		1 31 0

Continue with Parts 4 and 5 on Answer Sheet 2 ▶

UNIVERSITY *of* CAMBRIDGE
Local Examinations Syndicate

S A M P L E

Candidate Name
If not already printed write name
in CAPITALS and complete the
Candidate No. grid (in pencil)

Candidate's signature ....

Examination Title

Centre

  Supervisor:

  if the candidate is ABSENT or has WITHDRAWN shade here ▭

Centre No.

Candidate No.

Examination Details

0	0	0	0
1	1	1	1
2	2	2	2
3	3	3	3
4	4	4	4
5	5	5	5
6	6	6	6
7	7	7	7
8	8	8	8
9	9	9	9

Answer sheet 2

Part 4

32	....	32 0 1 2
33	....	33 0 1 2
34	....	34 0 1 2
35	....	35 0 1 2
36	....	36 0 1 2
37	....	37 0 1 2
38	....	38 0 1 2
39	....	39 0 1 2

Part 5

40		40
40	....	0 1 2
41	....	41 0 1 2
42	....	42 0 1 2
43	....	43 0 1 2

Part 5: question 44

For Examiner use only

Examiner number:
Team and Position

Marks

Content	0	1	2	3	4

Language	0	1.1	1.2	2.1	2.2	3.1	3.2	4.1	4.2	5.1	5.2

0	0	0	0
1	1	1	1
2	2	2	2
3	3	3	3
4	4	4	4
5	5	5	5
6	6	6	6
7	7	7	7
8	8	8	8
9	9	9	9

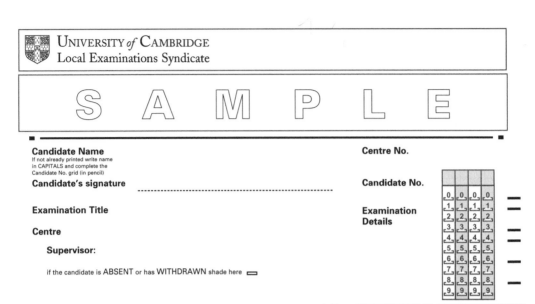

Candidate Answer Sheet

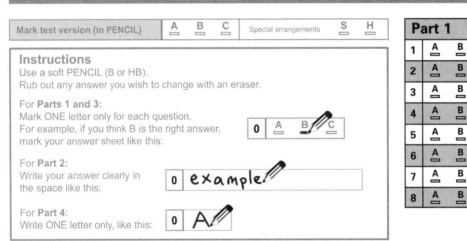

Part 1			
1	A	B	C
2	A	B	C
3	A	B	C
4	A	B	C
5	A	B	C
6	A	B	C
7	A	B	C
8	A	B	C

Part 2		Do not write here
9		1 9 0
10		1 10 0
11		1 11 0
12		1 12 0
13		1 13 0
14		1 14 0
15		1 15 0
16		1 16 0
17		1 17 0

Part 3				
18	A	B	C	D
19	A	B	C	D
20	A	B	C	D
21	A	B	C	D
22	A	B	C	D

Part 4		Do not write here
23		1 23 0
24		1 24 0
25		1 25 0
26		1 26 0
27		1 27 0
28		1 28 0